Berlitz®
Gran Canaria

Text by Pam Barrett
Photography: Gregory Wrona and
Gary John Norman
Cover photograph by Gary John Norman/Apa
Layout Concept: Klaus Geisler
Picture Editor: Hilary Genin
Managing Editor: Tony Halliday

Berlitz POCKET
GUIDE

Gran Canaria

First Edition 2004

PHOTOGRAPHY
Pam Barrett 35, 39, 45, 46, 67; Chris Coe/Berlitz 6, 24; Gary John Norman/Apa 8, 19, 21, 26, 32, 42, 43, 49, 50, 56, 63, 64, 66, 72, 76, 82, 87, 88, 89, 92, 98; Mark Read/Apa 13, 33; Roger Tidman/NHPA 9; Gregory Wrona/Apa 11, 12, 20, 28, 30, 34, 36, 47, 55, 57, 59, 60, 61, 68, 71, 74, 75, 82, 91, 95, 100.

CONTACTING THE EDITORS
Every effort has been made to provide accurate information in this publication, but changes are inevitable. The publisher cannot be responsible for any resulting loss, inconvenience or injury. We would appreciate it if readers would call our attention to any errors or outdated information by contacting Berlitz Publishing, PO Box 7910, London SE1 1WE, England. Fax: (44) 20 7403 0290;
e-mail: berlitz@apaguide.co.uk
www.berlitzpublishing.com

Puerto de Mogán
(page 54), one of
the prettiest places
on the island, a
perfect blend of
tradition and
tourism

Towering Roque
Nublo (page 74)
has become a
symbol of
Gran Canaria
◀

The stone Cruz de Tejeda
(page 73) marks one of the
highest points on the island
▼

*Printed in Singapore by Insight Print Services (Pte) Ltd, 38 Joo Koon Road, Singapore 628990.
Tel: (65) 6865-1600. Fax: (65) 6861-6438*

*Berlitz Trademark Reg. U.S. Patent Office
and other countries. Marca Registrada*

TOP TEN ATTRACTIONS

Casa de Colón (page 31) is one of the finest traditional buildings in Las Palmas

There are stunning views from the Mirador del Balcón (page 60) on the rocky west coast

The lively Playa de las Canteras (page 36) is a popular city beach

The pristine Maspalomas dunes (page 50) are like a desert by the sea

Teror (page 70) is a pretty town with a long history

Puerto de las Nieves (page 60) is the place to go for excellent fish

A road through the lush Barranco de Guayadeque (page 43)

CONTENTS

A ➤ in the text denotes a highly recommended sight

Fact Sheets

INTRODUCTION

The Canary Islands have always been regarded as a bridge between continents. They were the last stopping-off point for Columbus on his journey of discovery in 1492, when emergency repairs were done in Las Palmas to one of his three ships. During the 16th and 17th centuries, the islands were important trading centres through which passed much of the profitable sea traffic between Spain and the Americas. Latin American influences are still visible, in the food and the language, while the architecture reminds us that these were Spanish colonies at a time when the peninsula was at its most wealthy and powerful.

The archipelago lies in the Atlantic Ocean, some 1,100km (700 miles) southwest of mainland Spain and comprises the islands of Gran Canaria, Lanzarote and Fuerteventura to the east, and Tenerife, La Gomera, La Palma and El Hierro to the west. Gran Canaria, the third largest island, is some 195km (120 miles) from the African mainland, on a level with southern Morocco. The island is circular in shape and covers an area of 1,532 sq km (592 sq miles).

Landscape, Wildlife and Climate

Gran Canaria was formed some 16 million years ago by volcanic activity beneath the Atlantic, at a point where continental drift made the ocean bed particularly unstable. The central mountain massif was once a volcano, and the gorges *(barrancos)* radiating from it were formed by the subsequent process of erosion. Although the island is so small, it is extremely diverse. The eastern side is lush and fertile; the north and west somewhat bleak and barren; while the stretches

Roque Nublo, with Tenerife's Mt Teide in the distance

of white sand dunes in the south, barely populated until the 1960s, are now the island's holiday playground. Coastal roads in the west are winding and vertiginous, with stunning views, while away from the coast, all roads lead upwards. The highest point is the Pico de las Nieves – Peak of the Snows – at 1,949m (6,394ft).

Vegetation on Gran Canaria is as varied as the landscape. The fire-resistant Canary pine *(Pinus canariensis)* rules over the mountainous zone, while a pink rock rose *(Cistus symphytifolius)* clusters around its feet, and varieties of thyme, sage and broom scent the air. The Canary Island spurge *(Euphorbia canariensis)* survives well in the dry southern region, as does tajinaste *(Echium decaisnei),* a kind of borage, and the Cardon cactus *(Pachycereus pringlei),* while southern valleys support verdant groves of date palms *(Phoenix canariensis).* Prickly pear *(Opuntia ficus indica)* is seen all over the northern and central areas; imported from Mexico in the 16th century, it was used to cultivate the cochineal beetle. The most unusual vegetation is the dragon tree *(Dracaena draco),* which got its name from its red resin known as dragon's blood; this ancient survivor is mostly seen in botanical gardens. The plants you notice immedi-

Prickly pears will grow in the most inhospitable terrain

ately – brilliant bougainvillaea, hibiscus and poinsettia, clambering over walls
and brightening parks and
gardens – are not indigenous
but were brought to the
islands from subtropical
parts and have flourished in
the equable climate.

Island birds include the
indigenous blue chaffinch
(*pinzón* in Spanish); green-
finches – not indigenous but
very happy here – greater-

**The shy Canary chat is an
indigenous island bird**

spotted woodpeckers in the pine forests; the shy Canary chat;
and canaries. These are not the bright yellow we are accus-
tomed to, but little dun-coloured creatures, which changed
colour when they were caged and their breeding controlled.
However, the wild ones sing as sweetly as their caged cousins.

Gran Canaria has year-round sunshine – some 300 days a
year in the south. A strange grey haze called the *panza de
burro* – donkey's belly – sometimes affects the north. Winter
temperatures average 22–24°C (72–75°F), summer averages
are 26–28°C (79–82°F), although they often exceed 30°C
(86°F). High season is November to April, but July and
August are also popular with Spanish visitors and, despite
the heat, with English and German families, taking advan-
tage of the long school holidays.

People and Language

Gran Canaria is part of the Spanish Autonomous Region of
the Canary Islands *(see page 19)*. The population numbers
760,000, of whom 364,000 live in the capital, Las Palmas.
They are, on the whole, relaxed, open-minded people, but

keen to stress that they are *canarios*, first and foremost. Mainland Spaniards they refer to as *'los peninsulares'*.

Spanish (*castellano*) is the language of the islands. However, there are differences from the peninsula, many of which reflect the two-way traffic between the Canaries and Latin America. Final consonants are swallowed and 'z' is pronounced 's', as in the Americas, rather than the lisped 'th' of mainland Spain. A number of Latino words have been borrowed, too: a bus is a *guagua* and potatoes are *papas*. The strong English influence on the islands *(see page 18)* has also left some linguistic traces: a cake is a *queque*, and a traditional Canarian knife is a *naife*.

There is a large expatriate population – chiefly English and German – many of whom came for holidays and either bought retirement homes or opened bars or restaurants. The official religion is Catholic, although Anglican, Muslim, Mormon and other religions have a presence.

Most of the numerous traditional festivals on the island have religious origins. The wild pre-lent carnival stands out

> Carnival began as a religious event, a last celebration before the lean days of Lent, and developed into a riotous affair, with lavish processions and costumed balls. Carnival takes place throughout the Catholic world and the huge ones in Gran Canaria and Tenerife are usually staggered so they do not take place at exactly the same time.

– a time of elaborate parades, gorgeous costumes and riotous behaviour – but there are other fascinating ones, including the fiesta of the Virgen del Carmen, when the patron saint of the sea is honoured in the majority of ports; the Bajada de las Ramas in Puerto de las Nieves; and the hugely popular mix of religious and secular celebrations for the Virgen del Pino in Teror *(see page 70)*.

Tourism is the mainstay of the island's economy

Economy and Environment

Traditionally, the island's economy has been dependent on agriculture, from sugar cane in the 16th century to cochineal, to bananas and, more recently, tomatoes. Gran Canaria's principal source of employment today is in the service sector, of which tourism is a major part. EU funds have been used to strengthen the island infrastructure – roads, airports and hospitals. The islands all suffer from a water shortage, a problem intensified by the strain that so many visitors place on the system, but this has been partly overcome by the creation of these desalination plants, some fuelled by wind power.

In an attempt to break away from the sun, sand and sangria image of the islands, a large amount has also gone into the *turismo rural* initiative, whereby traditional buildings are converted into rural hotels in areas of great natural beauty, providing a peaceful base for walkers and nature lovers.

Reasons to Visit

Although many people come to Gran Canaria for the sun and sand, there is a great deal more on offer. Las Palmas is a true capital city with a vibrant cultural life. There is a splendid auditorium, a new theatre, some excellent restaurants, lively nightlife in the clubs and bars, and numerous good museums. The central mountainous region of the island, crowned by the Pico de las Nieves, is stunningly beautiful and offers great opportunities for walking and climbing, and the northern towns of Arucas and Teror have delightful historic centres with traditional architecture. The *barrancos* (gorges) are lush with tropical vegetation. The south is ideal for boating and water sports of all kinds, with craft and equipment available for hire; and, a very short distance from the brash resorts, the vast and empty dunes of Maspalomas feel like a desert by the sea.

The dunes of Maspalomas

A BRIEF HISTORY

Much of the Canary Islands' history between their conquest in the late 15th-century and the present is tied up with that of the Spanish mainland. As a vital point for trade with the Americas, Gran Canaria briefly shared in the prosperity of Spain's Golden Age, although it suffered economic decline thereafter. And in the late 20th century, the islands, along with Spain, became part of the European Union. But long before the Spaniards ever set foot here, there was a flourishing civilisation.

Land of the Brave

Tamarán – land of the brave – was the proud name given to Gran Canaria by the Guanches, the pre-Hispanic people of the islands. No one is quite sure where the Guanches came from. Some historians and scientists think they were related to the Canarii tribe, who lived on the Saharan side of the Atlas Mountains. The few fragments of writing that can be reconstructed are similar to scripts used by the ancient Berber people, and some Canarian place names are similar too. But as far as can be deduced, the Guanches had no boats, so how they crossed from the African coast remains a mystery. Perhaps, having settled on the islands, they simply forgot how to sail.

Quite a lot has been discovered about the culture of

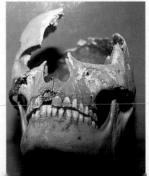

A Guanche skull in the Museo Canario, Las Palmas

these original islanders. Language and social structure varied from island to island. On Gran Canaria, the rulers were called *guanartemes* and shared some of their power with a *faycan*, who combined the role of judge and priest. Next on the social ladder came the aristocracy, the *guayres*.

The Guanches were a settled, agricultural people, who lived in groups of caves. *Gofio*, toasted flour originally made from barley, was their staple, but, as well as roots, they could pick a variety of wild fruits and berries. Pigs, sheep and goats provided meat as well as the materials for shelters, containers and clothes, and milk also came from sheep and goats. Fish formed a part of their diet, even when they had to travel some distance down to the coast to find it.

The Guanches did not have the wheel, they knew nothing of metalworking and did not use bows and arrows. Their domestic implements were made from stone and bone or

The Canary Islands were shown on the 14th-century Catalan Atlas

from obsidian, a black, volcanic glass. Porous lava was made into millstones and mortars. Their vessels and containers were made from pottery, wood, leather and woven cane. They mummified their dead and buried them in caves or stone-lined graves, and it is evidence from mummies so far discovered that has led scientists to place the original islanders' ethnic origins in northwest Africa. The Museo Canario has a number of mummies and skulls in its collection, along with domestic items, remarkably well preserved in the dry climate.

The Conquerors Arrive

The first conquering force, in 1403, was led by a Norman lord, Jean de Béthencourt, and funded by the king of Castile, but he failed to take the two main prizes – Gran Canaria and Tenerife. It wasn't until 1478 that another attempt was made, under the aegis of the Catholic Monarchs – Ferdinand and Isabella – of a newly united Spain. As the force was undermanned and the indigenous people put up quite a fight, it took several years to subdue them. Pedro de Vera was the man for the job. Arriving as military governor in 1480 he is said to have killed Doramas, the most warlike of the chiefs, with his own hands on the Montaña de Arucas. This coup, and the capture and conversion two years later of chief Tenesor Semidan brought the native people under control, but not before many of them had been killed, starved to death or committed ritual suicide.

De Vera remained governor for 10 years, during which time, in the interests of security, he had many of the local population deported or enslaved. This, together with an influx of European farmers and entrepreneurs, plus two severe outbreaks of plague, meant that within half a century the indigenous population was outnumbered. Those who survived had been forcibly 'converted' and many had intermarried with the incomers.

Prosperity and Decline

Because of their location, the Canary Islands became a proving ground for future Spanish colonisation strategies in the Americas. These revolved around slavery and sugar cane, both of which were were introduced to the Americas from the Canaries. The sugar boom on the Canaries only lasted until the mid-16th century, when competition from Brazil and the Caribbean became too strong. While Tenerife was able to switch to a lucrative wine industry, conditions on Gran Canaria were unsuitable for viniculture and the island became something of a poor relation, locked in fierce rivalry with flourishing Tenerife, which became the residence of the Captain-General and location of the first university.

The problems Gran Canaria suffered during the 16th and 17th centuries were intensified by the fact that the island and her ships were frequently attacked by pirates. The worst outrage was in 1599, when the Dutch buccaneer Pieter van der Does sacked and burned Las Palmas.

Gran Canaria began to assert its independence – from Tenerife and mainland Spain – in 1808 when the Napoleonic Wars destroyed Tenerife's wine trade. A junta was formed in Las Palmas, calling for 'a patriotic government, independent of the peninsula', but it was unsuccessful. Not until the 1860s did the island's fortunes begin to recover, with the introduction of cochineal, the red dye produced from a beetle of the same name that feeds on cacti. The boom was short-lived, as the invention of cheaply produced aniline

> **The Bishop's Palace in Las Palmas was one notable victim of van der Does' attack; another was the capital's Catedral de Santa Ana. In a display case in the cathedral today there is a splendid bell, a gift from the Asociación Nederlandesa-Canaria in 1999, 500 years after the privateer destroyed the original.**

The Catedral de Santa Ana suffered during raids by Dutch pirates

dyes brought a virtual end to the industry. Poverty and unemployment forced many islanders to emigrate to the Americas, mainly Cuba and Venezuela.

It was only in the 1880s that things really began to get better, largely due to Fernando León y Castillo, a local politician who became foreign minister in the Spanish government. With the collaboration of his brother, Juan, an engineer, he embarked on a project to transform Las Palmas into the major port on the island. Within about six years, the Puerto de la Luz was dealing with most of the steamship trade that passed through the islands.

War and Recovery
The last of the briefly successful monocultures was bananas, introduced by the British in the late 19th century. But World War I had a disastrous effect on the trade, thereby creating more poverty and more emigration. Contact with the New

World, where Cuba had won freedom from Spain in 1898, led to calls for Canarian independence, but most people simply wanted the division of the archipelago into two separate provinces. Formalisation of this came in 1927 but no new economic solutions had been found when the three-year Spanish Civil War began in 1936, initiated by Francisco Franco, military governor of the Canary Islands. He spent

British Interests

There is a street in Las Palmas called Alfredo Jones, another called Tomás Miller, and the science museum is the Museo Elder. They were named after three of the British businessmen who had the most influence on Las Palmas in the 19th and early 20th centuries. There was a fourth – James Swanton – who seems to have been overlooked when street names were given out. British influence on the island was far reaching. Swanton and his young cousin, Thomas Miller, ran an import-export business, started in the 1820s. It flourished at the height of the cochineal boom and when aniline dyes killed demand, Miller began importing coal from Cardiff. The Santa Catalina jetty in the new port was financed by a second generation of Millers and Swantons; major shipping lines with offices in the port were British owned – one was the Elder-Dempster Line, in whose premises the Museo Elder is housed; and the water, electricity and telephone services were all set up by Englishmen. Sir Alfred Jones never lived on the island, but he founded the Grand Canary Coaling Company and financed the construction of the Hotel Santa Catalina. These wealthy businessmen established the British Club (still in Calle León y Castillo) and founded the first golf club. They built houses in the leafy Ciudad Jardín (Garden City) in Las Palmas and on the hills outside, in Tafira and Santa Brígida, still regarded as extremely desirable places to live. For several decades at least, Gran Canaria was an informal colony of the British Empire.

the last night before launching his coup in the Hotel Madrid in Las Palmas. (The Canaries are the only parts of Spain where you will still see main streets named 'Generalissimo Franco' or 'Primo de Rivera', the latter after a Falangist leader executed in 1936.)

After the civil war and World War II, the Canaries, like the rest of Spain, initially suffered from isolation

Agriculture is still a labour-intensive activity

and economic hardship. Things improved a little in the 1950s, when Spain was once more recognised by the international community, but it was the advent of tourism in the following decade that really turned the tide. Franco remained in power until his death in 1975, when his authoritarian regime was replaced by democratic government. The new Spanish Constitution of 1978 created the Autonomous Region of the Canary Islands – now one of 17 such regions. The archipelago is not completely separate from Spain but the island government, the Cabildo Insular, does have a great deal of freedom.

The islands have enjoyed considerable commercial freedom and tax exemptions ever since the 19th century, but when Spain became a full member of the European Union, fiscal changes had to be introduced. In order to protect trade and industry the Puerto de la Luz and the industrial area round Arinaga were confirmed as a Free Trade Zone, governed by a local consortium.

The economy is not too unhealthy, but it needs some support. The agricultural sector finds it difficult to compete in the wider market. Until the end of 1995, Spain guaranteed a

Mass tourism changed the face of Gran Canaria

market for Gran Canaria's bananas but since then, despite EU subsidies, the industry has been uneconomical. Production costs are high and bananas need a lot of water – a scarce commodity. The island is a major producer of tomatoes for the European market, but countries with lower labour costs, such as Morocco, have been able to undercut the Canarian growers. The only real money-spinner is tourism.

Tourism and the Environment

The creation of the resorts of San Agustín, Playa del Inglés and Maspalomas in the 1960s, catering to sun-seeking northern Europeans, changed the face of Gran Canaria. This, together with the opening of Gando international airport in 1974, made tourism the main industry. The economy benefited enormously, and islanders gained employment, for most of the year at least, but inevitably there were effects on the environment. Hotels, swimming pools and golf courses are problematic for an island with a water shortage. Heavy traffic took its toll on the roads. And the island's reputation as a holiday destination suffered, too, from the alcohol-fuelled antics of some tourists.

For ecological and economic reasons, the Cabildo Insular has made huge efforts to diversify the tourist industry and protect the environment. Many areas have been designated natural parks and special nature reserves; in fact, over 66,000 hectares (154,00 acres), some 40 percent of the island, is protected to some degree. Active environmental protection groups exert a steadying influence.

At present all traffic going from one end of the island to the other goes through Las Palmas, creating horrendous traffic problems. To alleviate this, a new motorway network is under construction – parts are already open – which will take traffic around rather than through Las Palmas and relieve the chronic congestion.

Wind and Water

Water on the island is not only in short supply but, until recently, had been in the hands of private suppliers. This has always been a contentious issue, and in the south it has been taken out of private hands and is run by a franchise called Eléctrica Maspalomas. Water shortages have been alleviated to some extent by desalination plants – there's a huge one south of Las Palmas – but they are extremely expensive if they are run off the

Water is a scarce resource that must be handled carefully

national grid, so wind power has been introduced to keep costs down. The huge wind farm at Pozo Izquierdo on the gusty east coast is the foremost example of this.

A Gentler Image

In recent years Gran Canaria's tourist industry has been given a new direction, with less emphasis on sun, sea, sand and more on other aspects of the island. EU funds have helped in the promotion of the *turismo rural* initiative – creating country hotels and helping convert traditional buildings into holiday accommodation. The opening up of the *caminos reales* (royal paths) in the island's interior are part of the drive to attract walkers and people with a love of the countryside.

There has also been a resurgence of interest in the pre-Hispanic past, and in rediscovering the island's cultural heritage, and a number of books have been published on the subject. Many people claim to be directly descended from the Guanches. In Gáldar, one of the two ancient capitals, which calls itself the Ciudad de los Guanartemes (City of Rulers), most of the streets have indigenous names. An increasing number of children are being given Guanche names, such as Tamara or Tenesor, and a favoured name for bars and restaurants is Tagoror, which means a place of assembly. Perhaps this is all part of move to establish a new sense of island identity, while still being very much a part of Europe.

Children will grow up to be both islanders and Europeans

Historical Landmarks

circa **1st–2nd centuries** BC Guanche settlements in Canary Islands.

AD1477–83 Spanish force lands on the island and subdues Guanches.

1492 Columbus briefly stops at Las Palmas before sailing west and discovering America.

circa **1500** Sugar cane introduced and African slaves imported. From 1554, the sugar industry declines.

1700–1950 Poverty forces many islanders to emigrate to Latin America.

1830 A short economic boom follows the introduction of the cochineal beetle. Prosperity ended by invention of aniline dyes.

1852 Isabella II declares the Canary Islands a Free Trade Zone.

1890 The British introduce bananas as a monoculture.

1911 Self-administration council – Cabildo Insular – introduced.

1927 The Canary Islands are divided in two. Santa Cruz de Tenerife becomes capital of the western province, and Las Palmas de Gran Canaria of the eastern.

1936 Franco, military governor of the Canary Islands, initiates the three-year Spanish Civil War.

1956 The first charter plane lands on Gran Canaria. Tourism rapidly develops into the most important industry.

1974 Gando international airport opens.

1978–82 New Spanish Constitution joins the two island provinces to form the Autonomous Region of the Canary Islands.

1986 Spain joins the European Union and negotiates a special status for the Canary Islands.

1995 Islands integrated into the EU but retain important tax privileges.

1996 In national elections, the Coalición Canaria, a union of regional parties, takes four seats in Madrid parliament.

2000 Some 3½ million people a year are visiting Gran Canaria.

2002 The euro becomes the national currency.

2003 Partido Popular makes electoral gains, mainly due to charismatic leader, former Las Palmas mayor, José María Soria.

WHERE TO GO

Gran Canaria is not a large island, but if you travel the short distance from the capital, Las Palmas, to the dunes of Maspalomas in the south, explore the lush Barranco de Agaete in the northwest, scale the mountainous central heights, or spend a peaceful day in one of the pretty fishing ports, you will feel that you have visited a small continent.

LAS PALMAS

Las Palmas, capital of Gran Canaria, is a sprawling city with a population of 364,000 people, nearly 80 percent of whom make their living in the service industries. There are several distinct focal points. To the south is the historical centre, Vegueta, which was declared a UNESCO World Heritage Site in 1990. A busy dual carriageway divides Vegueta from the attractive old shopping district of Triana, with its cafés and art-nouveau buildings. The traffic-filled Avenida Marítima and the noisy stretch of Calle León y Castillo lead to the next points of interest: lush Parque Doramas and the Muelle Deportivo, the yacht harbour. A further busy stretch, either following the sea or on a parallel road inland, leads to the huge Puerto de la Luz and lively Parque Santa Catalina. From here, a grid of streets links the city and the beach, Playa de las Canteras, which made Las Palmas a holiday resort before those in the south existed.

Between these points are the busy commercial streets around Avenida Mesa y López, the select Ciudad Jardín, where flowers blossom in walled gardens and government buildings fly their flags. At the far northern tip is La Isleta, a working-class district with some excellent fish restaurants; and up on

Puerto de Mogán is one of the island's prettiest little ports

The art nouveau kiosk in Parque San Telmo

the hills behind, is the Ciudad Alta where many of the capital's citizens live and work.

Triana

Whether you come straight from the airport or on a bus trip from the south, you will probably arrive at **Parque San Telmo**, for this is the site of the city's main (underground) bus terminal and the place where taxis wait to deliver passengers to other parts of town. There's a children's playground in the square – it isn't really a park – and a pretty little chapel, the Ermita de San Telmo, whitewashed and simple outside, ornate and gilded within. Opposite, an art-nouveau kiosk, decorated with gleaming tiles, serves drinks at tables under towering *fisco* trees. At the back of the square, a wall plaque on a military building announces that here, on 18 July 1936, General Franco announced the coup that initiated the three-year Spanish Civil War.

To the left of the square, the paved, pedestrianised **Calle Mayor de Triana** has several attractive facades – some colonial in style, some art nouveau – and a medley of shops, ranging from a tiny fabric store and old-fashioned tobacconists, to branches of Zara and Marks & Spencer. Off to the right, in narrow, pretty streets reminiscent of the Triana district in Seville from which this area took its name, are smart boutiques and a few antiques and gift shops. The Librería del Cabildo Insular on the corner of Cano and Travieso, has a wide choice of books and maps on the islands.

Calle Cano is also the place to find the **Casa-Museo Pérez Galdós** (open Mon–Fri 9am–7pm, sometimes Sat–Sun 10am–2pm; guided visits on the hour; free). The building where the novelist was born in 1843 *(see panel below)* is a splendid example of Canary Island architecture, built around a courtyard and furnished with portraits and items from his houses in Madrid and Santander, many of which he designed and made himself. The conducted tours are in Spanish only, but are worth taking, simply to appreciate the house.

Close by is a little jewel of a square, the **Plazoleta de Cairasco**. The Hotel Madrid, one of the oldest in the city, serves meals and drinks at tables out under the palms till late at night. At the north end, the splendid **Gabinete Literario**, floodlit after dark, is an art nouveau treasure designated a 'Monumento Histórico Artístico'. Once a theatre, it is now home to a literary society, but it houses a restaurant/café with comfortable chairs on a shady terrace.

Famous Son

Benito Pérez Galdós (1843–1920) is widely regarded as one of the greatest Spanish novelists and playwrights, and many believe he would have received the Nobel Prize for Literature had it not been for his unpopular political views. His books and plays offer an inside view of Spanish life, and he was unusual in that he did not restrict himself to the world of just one social class. Born in Las Palmas, he spent much of his life in Madrid and Santander, where he became increasingly involved with politics. A staunch republican, he was elected as a senator for Madrid in 1910, and for Las Palmas when he returned in 1914. His greatest play, *Electra*, received its premier in the theatre named after him, an ochre-coloured, art nouveau building in Triana, currently closed for renovation.

To the side of the little plaza runs the **Alameda de Colón**, at the north end of which, near a bust of Columbus, is the whitewashed, colonial-style **Iglesia de San Francisco**. Destroyed in the fire of 1599, following Pieter van de Does' attack, it was rebuilt during the 17th century, then became a parochial church after the monks were ejected (as they were throughout Spain in 1821). At the south end of the *alameda* (which means a tree-lined avenue) in an imposing building with stone-framed doorways, is a cultural centre, known by the acronym CICCA, where La Caja de las Canarias, a munificent savings bank, funds exhibitions, films, music and theatrical performances.

You are close now to the major highway (Calle Juan de Quesada) that separates Triana from Vegueta, but before you cross there's another attractive square. It is officially called Hurtado de Mendoza, after an early 20th-century painter, but

The Plaza de las Ranas is a shady spot in a busy city

usually known as **Las Ranas** (The Frogs) because the long pool that runs down the centre is fed by two spouting frogs. A nearby café of the same name, housed in the Monopol Commercial Centre and opposite an imposing library building, is always buzzing with students at night. The university is a short distance up the highway, and there is some student accommodation in Triana. The newish Monopol Centre itself houses a few shops and fast-food outlets, but is at present surprisingly under-used.

Vegueta

The historic centre of Las Palmas has a character all of its own. This was once the aristocratic quarter and its cobbled streets are lined with splendid colonial buildings with intricately carved balconies and intriguing, palm-filled courtyards, glimpsed when their huge, polished doors are ajar.

At its heart is the twin-towered **Catedral de Santa Ana** ◀ (open Mon–Fri 10am–4.30pm, Sat 10am–1.30pm; access only through Diocesan Museum; admission fee). Started in 1497, it wasn't completed until the 20th century and is a mixture of architectural styles – Gothic, Renaissance and neoclassical. Elements on the facade and many of the statues inside are the work of the Canary Island sculptor, José Luján Pérez (1756–1815).

The adjoining **Museo Diocesano de Arte Sacro** (same hours as cathedral; entrance in Calle Espíritu Santo) has a lovely cloister, the Patio de los Naranjos (Orange Trees), its peace interrupted only by birdsong. Among the sacred paintings and artefacts is an impressive modern series, *Stations of the Cross*, by local artist, Jesús Arencibia.

If you don't want to visit the museum and cathedral, you can always just take the modern lift (same hours as cathedral; admission fee), which will whisk you up to the top of one of the towers for a great view over the city.

The Casa de Colón is one of the city's most splendid buildings

Among the magnificent buildings in the **Plaza de Santa Ana**, the **Palacio Regental** may be the star. It is largely 17th century, although the facade dates from 1867. The Canarian balcony is older, as is the huge and splendid doorway, above which is the coat of arms of the kingdoms of León and Castile. Little remains of the adjoining **Palacio Episcopal** (Bishop's Palace) except an ornate single-storey facade. It was a victim of the fire of 1599, when Dutch privateer Pieter van der Does destroyed most of the town *(see page 16)*.

Huge bronze dogs, the island's heraldic animal, sit patiently outside the cathedral, and at the other end of the square is the elegant 19th-century building housing the **Casas Consistoriales** (Offices of Island Government), at present undergoing substantial renovation work.

Beyond the square, you come to the little Plaza Espíritu Santo, which has an unusual domed fountain in the centre. From here, Calle Dr Chil leads to the Museo Canario. This is a street of splendid houses with carved wooden balconies and intriguing, shady courtyards, most of which are now the homes and offices of lawyers.

Three Vegueta Museums

The first of three Vegueta museums that deserve attention is the **Museo Canario** (open Mon–Fri 10am–8pm, Sat–Sun 10am–2pm; admission fee) on Calle Dr Verneau. It houses the Canary Islands' largest collection of pre-Hispanic objects – pottery, tools, mummies and skeletons, and dozens of skulls, lined up in glass cases like macabre ornaments. Here you will see the ochre-coloured figure of the Idolo de Tara, a fertility goddess, copies of which are on sale in souvenir shops all over the island. There are also scale models of Guanche dwellings and a replica of the Cueva Pintada in Gáldar *(see page 64)*.

The **Casa de Colón** (open Mon–Fri 9am–7pm, Sat–Sun 9am–3pm; free) is an endearing little museum, with ornate doorways and beautiful latticed balconies. Colón is the Spanish name for Columbus and it is claimed, with no supporting evidence, that he stayed here while one of his ships was being repaired. There is a replica of the cabin of *La Niña*, one of Columbus' fleet, nautical maps and charts, a collection of pre-Columbian artefacts from Ecuador and Mexico, and two noisy parrots which rule the inner courtyard. The house was the birthplace, in 1927, of the operatic tenor Alfredo Kraus.

A plaque on the wall of San Antonio Abad, the tiny chapel next to the Casa de Colón, claims that the explorer stopped to pray on this spot before setting off on his voyage of discovery.

The **Centro Atlántico de Arte Moderno** (CAAM; open Tues–Sat 10am–9pm, Sun 10am–2pm; free) is worth visiting mainly because it is a wonderful exhibition space – white walls, marble stairs and acres of glass, concealed behind a traditional facade. It has a good reputation as an educational and cultural centre, but visitors may find its changing exhibitions are generally of less interest than the building itself. The museum also has a smaller venue in Plaza San Antonio Abad, close to the Casa de Colón.

Parque Doramas and the Pueblo Canario

Leave the old town now and get a bus (from Teatro Pérez Galdós on the Triana side of the highway, or from Parque San Telmo) to **Parque Doramas**, in a prosperous, leafy part of town known as the Ciudad Jardín. Amid tropical greenery in front of the ultra-smart **Hotel Santa Catalina**, a large statue dedicated to the vanquished chief Doramas shows aboriginal people leaping from a rocky fountain.

To the left of the hotel is the **Pueblo Canario**, a little complex of traditional island buildings with café tables in a central plaza. This Canarian village was designed in the 1930s by brothers Néstor and Miguel Fernández de la Torre,

Leaping Guanches in the lush Parque Doramas

to interest early tourists in island ways. Costumed folk dancing displays are held here every Sunday at 11.30am (free).

The **Museo Néstor** (open Tues–Sat 10am–8pm, Sun 10.30am–2.30pm; admission fee) dedicated to the better known of the brothers, is part of the complex. Born in Las Palmas, Néstor (1887–1938), always known simply by his first name,

Children share secrets in the Pueblo Canario

spent much of his life in Paris, Madrid and Barcelona, where he became famous for his sensuous paintings and imaginative stage designs. He returned to the island in later life with a heightened awareness of his roots and painted two series of works, *Atlantic Poem* and *Visiones de Gran Canaria*. Both can be seen in the museum, along with earlier works.

Opposite the park is the Club Natación Metropol swimming and sports club. Beside it, an underpass leads below the Avenida Marítima to the **Muelle Deportivo**, the yacht harbour, from where transatlantic yachtsmen set out, and visitors can take catamaran trips. There's a nautical bar here, the Match Cup, and a new promenade beside the water is soon to be lined with cafés and shops, which will make this a pleasant area that's protected from the traffic on the road above. Adjoining the harbour area is the smart Club Náutico followed by the Playa de Alcaravaneras, a stretch of beach mostly frequented by local families.

Parque Santa Catalina

If you want to do any shopping, head inland along broad Calle Mesa y López, where most of the big stores are found, including two branches of Spain's largest department store, El Corte Inglés. Otherwise, it's not far from here to the next point of interest, **Parque Santa Catalina**. Although dotted with palm trees and vivid flower beds, this, like San Telmo, is more of a square than a park, but much bigger and busier. There is always a sense of activity here, with visitors and local people frequenting the outdoor cafés; crowds of elderly men playing chess, dominos and cards under specially-erected awnings; lottery ticket vendors calling to attract attention; and shoeshine men looking for customers. Here you can get local information from a small kiosk; board one of the open-topped, yellow *guagua turística* buses that allow you to hop on and off at sites of interest; make phone calls from

The Museo Elder keeps visitors entertained for hours

cabinas telefónicas at the north end of the square; surf the internet in an adjacent building; or book tickets in the Fred Olsen office for the ferry to Tenerife.

Around the Port

On the port side of the park is the striking **Museo Elder** (open Tues–Sun 10am–8pm; admission fee), a wonderful and well-organised science and technology museum. It

The new face of the Muelle Santa Catalina

is housed in a building that belonged to the Elder-Dempster Shipping Line, but has extended upwards and outwards. There are lots of interactive exhibits to amuse children, as well an industrial robot spot-welding a car, a model of Foucault's pendulum; an incubator where patient visitors can watch chicks hatching from eggs; and an IMAX cinema.

A landscaped pedestrian area leads from the museum to the **Muelle Santa Catalina**, in front of which an enormous, sail-like awning conceals nothing more exciting than the city's new, subterranean bus terminal. To the left of it, a shiny new commercial centre in brilliant shades of blue and yellow, **El Muelle**, overlooks the port. With numerous big-name stores, cinemas, discos and open-air restaurants and cafés, it is being promoted as a way of bringing new life, and new consumers, to this part of town.

Playa de las Canteras

The stretch northwards from here along the **Puerto de la Luz** is all industrial buildings and traffic-clogged roads, so cross back to Parque Santa Catalina and make your way, via

Calle Luís Morote, through a maze of streets, where shops specialise in watches, cameras, mobile phones and all things electrical, and car-hire outlets, hotels and restaurants proliferate. Suddenly, you are on the other side of what has now become a narrow peninsula, and arrive at the beach.

Playa de las Canteras is the 3-km (2-mile) stretch of white sand that made the city Gran Canaria's very first tourist resort. It is lined with hotels and restaurants, some smart, some a little flaky, and some of which have been here since the 1960s heyday. A wide promenade runs the length of the beach, dotted with palms and the sun umbrellas that restaurants set out by the sea and bright with the vivid clothes of African traders who set up their stalls here, selling carvings and jewellery. There is a constant parade of people – visitors in beach gear, local people more formally dressed, street entertainers and occasional beggars.

Playa de las Canteras is a locals' beach as well as a place for tourists

These days the beach is more popular with visiting mainland Spaniards than with northern Europeans and they use it to the full, forming circles to play bingo and setting up tables on which they lay out large picnic lunches. Ball games are forbidden during the day, but in the evening stretches of the beach become a football pitch. The natural reef, **La Barra**, a few hundred metres out, turns this stretch of coast into a natural lagoon, safe for children and non-swimmers.

Beach Extremities

At the north end of the beach (where the peninsula is at its narrowest), old wooden fishing boats are pulled up on the sand. On the windy point jutting out to sea, La Puntilla, there is a good fish restaurant. If you follow the road behind it you will reach the old fishermen's quarter of La Isleta. The main reason to come here is to scale the highest peak at **Las Coloradas** for a sweeping view of the sea, the mountains and the city – and to eat in El Padrino *(see page 136)*. It's a long, steep climb, though, and you would do better to take a taxi or a No. 41 bus from Parque Santa Catalina.

At the southern end of Playa de las Canteras, beyond the reef's protective arm and where the sands are darker, constant on-shore winds make ideal conditions for surfers. Once neglected, this end of Las Canteras is now being smartened up, with a landscaped promenade leading to the **Auditorio Alfredo Kraus**, home to the Las Palmas Philharmonic Orchestra *(see page 93)*. A mammoth bronze statue of the tenor, who was born in the city, stands proudly outside. Seen from a distance, the sand-coloured building appears to rise from the sea, and in some lights blends into the hills behind. Adjoining it is the stark Palacio de Congresos conference centre and, across the road, the city's biggest commercial centre, **Las Arenas**. From here, the arched bridge on the motorway heading north looks close enough to touch.

THE EAST

The lushest and loveliest part of Gran Canaria is the eastern region. It encompasses the verdant Barranco de Guayadeque, where there is still a small community of people living in caves, and several towns with delightful, well-preserved historic centres. It also includes the area around Arinaga, where strong winds enable world championship windsurfing competitions to be held and Pozo Izquierdo, Gran Canaria's biggest wind farm, to produce energy.

Driving down the motorway (the GC-1) from the airport or from Las Palmas, you will not be aware of the treasures that lie only a few kilometres inland. Faceless as most motorways, it is lined with factory buildings, out-of-town megastores and an airforce base, all set in a bare, scrubby landscape. It is, of course, the fastest way to reach the areas of interest, but if you are not in a hurry, you could explore the area on minor roads.

Jardín Canario

If you take the Santa Brígida road (GC-110) to the southwest of Las Palmas you can include the **Jardín Canario** (open daily 9am–6pm; free) on your itinerary. If you just want to make an excursion from Las Palmas to the garden you can take bus Nos. 301 or 303 (in the direction of San Mateo). They leave every 15 minutes from the bus station in Parque San Telmo and the journey takes about 20 minutes. The botanical garden lies close to the suburb of Tafira Alta, where elegant,

> If you visit the Jardín Canario by bus, ask the driver to tell you when you get there, or else he may not stop. And be prepared to cross the dual carriageway by an elevated pedestrian bridge in order to catch the bus back into town.

One of the many species of Aeonium that flourish in the Jardín Canario

early 20th-century villas and beautiful gardens are only slightly marred by the never-ending flow of traffic. The Jardín Canario is delightful, although the stepped, cobbled paths may rule it out for those who have difficulty getting around; and some may wish that more of the fascinating specimens were identified.

The garden was established in 1952 by the Swedish botanist Eric R. Sventenius and is laid out along the steeply sloping side of a gorge. This can be crossed at one point by a wooden bridge to reach a flatter section where a cactus garden includes an amazing selection of specimens from all over the world, many introduced to the island from the Americas in the 17th century.

Just past the main entrance there are specimens of *Laurisilva* (bay laurel), which covered much of the island before the Spanish conquest but has long since been destroyed.

There is also an avenue of dragon trees *(Dracaena draco)*, which were once believed to have healing properties; and a grove of *Pinus canariensis*, the indigenous pine tree. Allow a good couple of hours to visit the garden, because it is quite extensive and there is so much to see. Just outside the main entrance gate is a restaurant, which has a good reputation for serving typical Canarian food.

Caldera de Bandama

Just past Tafira Alta and Monte Lentiscal (the two prosperous suburbs virtually run into each other) drivers can take a left turn to the **Caldera de Bandama**. The volcanic crater is 1km (½ mile) wide and 200m (655ft) deep, and the best view of it is from the volcanic peak next door, the Pico de Bandama (574m/1,883ft), which has an observation platform and small bar – and you can drive to it. From here you also get magnificent views of the entire north and east coasts of the island. On a clear day you can sometimes see the neighbouring island of Fuerteventura to the northeast, while to the west looms the central massif.

Adventurous visitors can climb down into the crater itself, via a steep path that is visible from the rim – it takes about 30 minutes. At the bottom is an abandoned farmhouse, shaded by two enormous eucalyptus trees, and the outlines of terraced fields where vines were once cultivated.

South of the caldera, which is the Spanish word for cauldron but has become the international geological term for a volcanic crater, lies the largest golf course on the island – and the oldest one in Spain – the Real Club de Golf de Las Palmas, which was founded at the end of the 19th century by some of the English expatriates who were so influential in the growth and prosperity of the city, and who wanted to be able to indulge in one of their favourite forms of recreation.

Telde

Back on the main road, turn left at San José on the CG-80 to Telde. Follow signs to San Juan or the Centro Histórico and park as soon as you can, because Telde, the second-largest town on the island, is bedevilled by narrow, one-way streets and far too much traffic. There is a large modern section that is of little interest to visitors, but the old town, a protected conservation area since 1981, is well worth a stop. It centres on the attractive Plaza de San Juan, shaded by mature trees and surrounded by colonial-style houses with beautiful mosaic tiles and intricately carved balconies. Lording it over the square is the **Iglesia de San Juan Bautista** (open daily from 5pm). Building began in 1519, but the neo-Gothic towers are early 20th-century additions. It houses a beautiful 16th-century Flemish altarpiece showing six scenes from the life of the Virgin, acquired when the town grew rich from the

One of Telde's elegant mansions

sugar trade. Unfortunately, the altarpiece is so valuable that the church is usually only open during services and for a while afterwards, when a guardian is available. The church's other treasure is an image of Christ made in Mexico from corn cobs. Just off the square is a small children's park, with brightly-coloured birds in an aviary.

The street that links San Juan with the other historic district, San Fernando, is named, like many others in Gran Canaria, after Fernando and Juan León y Castillo, the brothers who transformed the port of Las Palmas *(see page 17)*. They were born in Telde and their home is now the **Casa-Museo León y Castillo** (open Mon–Fri 9am–1pm; free).

Cuatro Puertas

Telde was one of the two Guanche capitals before the Spanish arrived (Gáldar was the other) and the indigenous people have left us an interesting archaeological site, just off the GC-100 from Telde to Ingenio. **Cuatro Puertas** (always open; free), also known as Montaña Bermeja after the colour of its dark reddish stone, consists of a main chamber with

A model sugar mill erected in memory of Ingenio's past

four huge entrances. A shallow, semicircular enclave in the rock is thought to have been a sacrificial site, and the open space in front of the chamber was a *tagoror*, a place of assembly.

Ingenio

About 5km (3 miles) along the GC-100 lies the little town of **Ingenio**. As you approach you will see the **Museo de Piedras y Arte-**

sanía (Museum of Stones and Handicrafts; open Mon–Fri 8am–6pm; free). It's an attractive building and there are some pieces of agricultural machinery on show and a few glass cases displaying minerals, but it is really a shop selling embroidered linen, pottery and ornaments.

Ingenio itself is an attractive place, although you will be hard pressed to find a good place to eat. It was a prosperous sugar-refining centre in the 16th century (a model sugar press stands at the eastern approach to the town), but agriculture, chiefly tomato-growing, is the mainstay these days.

A good road through the Barranco de Guayadeque

Narrow alleys of whitewashed houses lead to the newly-tiled **Plaza de la Candelaria**, where modern fountains contrast with a white, colonial-style church and the ochre-coloured town hall. Beside the church, bronze statues of women washing clothes add interest to another fountain.

Barranco de Guayadeque

Just before you reach the next town, Agüimes, 2km (1 mile) away, you will see a sign to the **Centro de Interpretación de Guayadeque**, *see panel overleaf* (open Tues–Sat 9am–5pm, Sun 10am–6pm; admission fee). This is the best route to take to the **Barranco de Guayadeque**, well-surfaced and less tortuous than the one from Ingenio, which also leads to the interpretation centre. Now under a protection order, the *barranco* is one of the most beautiful valleys on the island. Its steep slopes are honeycombed with cave dwellings (*see below*), and lush flora still thrives – cacti, tajinaste, palms and poppies, among other plantlife. The *barrranco* is home to one of the biggest lizards in the world – the *Lagarto canarión*; sparrow hawks can be seen in the skies and the sound of woodpeckers is loud in the pine woods higher up. There are still several functioning wells in the gorge; the Morro Verano, at 170m/555ft, is the deepest.

The *barranco* is for serious walkers, and there is a reliable organisation in Agüimes that arranges hikes if you want to

Cave Dwellers

The Centro de Interpretación is a helpful introduction to the life of the valley and its people, and displays some of the items – pottery, bones and textiles – that have been recovered from caves. More items are on display in the Museo Canario in Las Palmas. The *barranco* was the most densely populated gorge on the island during Guanche times. Early inhabitants farmed the slopes and even went down to the coast to fish, as the remains of sea-snail and limpet shells indicate. Numerous grain stores have been excavated and many mumified bodies were found in caves when interest in the area was stimulated at the end of the 19th century. The cave villages that exist today are rapidly being depleted. In 1970, there were some 450 inhabitants, now there are only about 90 people. There are still two chapels, and a functioning school, although it has fewer than a dozen pupils. Some crops are still grown – potatoes and corn in the higher regions, almonds on the lower slopes and on the valley floor – and some goats, pigs and sheep are kept, but most people now work in bars and restaurants, catering to the tourists.

go with a group *(see page 86)*. If you go alone, make sure you have warm clothes for the chilly heights, strong shoes and plenty of water. However, there is much that can be enjoyed without doing anything too strenuous. The surfaced road continues for 9km (5 miles) or so beyond the Interpretation Centre, passing glorious scenery and reaching two cave villages, both still

One of Agüimes' statues, outside the Hotel de los Camellos

viable communities, with tiny chapels, a bar and rudimentary restaurant, and houses bright with geraniums. The road ends at the best-known cave restaurant, the Tagoror.

Agüimes

Agüimes is one of the most appealing towns on the island. It's a place where the Ayuntamiento (Town Hall) takes seriously the job of preserving and improving the environment, and fostering conservation-conscious tourism – and it shows. The outskirts of the town, where there is a bus station and a public swimming pool, is pleasant enough, but the **Casco Histórico** is the place to go.

Spotless, narrow streets of ochre- and terracotta-coloured houses – several of them converted into *casa rural* accommodation *(see pages 104 and 132)* – lead to the shady main square, **Plaza de Nuestra Señora del Rosario**. Here, and in other parts of town, a number of bronze statues have been erected, portraying rural life and local characters. The neoclassical **Iglesia de San Sebastián** (open daylight hours) at one end of the square, is a designated Monumento Histórico

Artístico and has works by island sculptor José Luján Pérez. The tourist office has an information centre with old photos and historical pieces. Classical music spills out from hidden speakers, a pretty café offers 'coffee and cake' and a wacky tapas bar, playing rap tapes, is something of an anomaly.

Wind turbines produce energy at Pozo Izquierdo

Arinaga

For a real contrast, make the short trip from Agüimes to **Arinaga**, a sleepy little place where graffiti indicates that local people are opposed to the planned extension of the port. As you will soon realise, this is a windy stretch of coast, but one much in favour with wind surfers, and since 2001 **Playa de Vargas** has been the venue for the annual PWA Windsurf Championships (in April/May). There is also a marine reserve and diving centre, at **Playa del Cabrón** *(see page 83)*, but what is most immediately obvious as you approach Arinaga are the huge, graceful and surprisingly quiet wind turbines producing energy at the Pozo Izquierdo plant.

THE SOUTHERN RESORTS

The southern resorts of Gran Canaria are synonymous with package holidays, where sun, sea and sand keep visitors happy by day, and discos and bars ensure the alcohol is flowing and the music thumping until the early hours of the morning. The resorts of San Agustín, Playa del Inglés and

Maspalomas, mini-cities built to provide instant gratification, were created out of this desert-by-the-sea *(see panel on page 48)* and therefore have no history, no corners where remnants of an earlier way of life linger on. What they do have is year-round, reliably good weather, miles of rolling sands, watersports facilities, hotels and apartments with lush gardens and landscaped swimming pools; and restaurants, clubs, bars and shops by the score.

To the west of the three main resorts lie Puerto Rico and Puerto de Mogán. The former is also an artificial creation, but smaller and more low-key than its neighbours, and with an emphasis on family entertainment and watersports of all kinds. The latter was a struggling little fishing village until the tourist boom began and has since been transformed into a delightful little resort built around a series of canals, with a wonderful sheltered harbour for yachtsmen.

Sun and shade beside the sea at Playa del Inglés

San Agustín

Whether you are coming direct from the airport, from Las Palmas, or from Agüimes, you will approach the resorts on the GC-1 motorway. The first one, **San Agustín**, was also the first to be built, in 1962. There is a plethora of hotels and apartment blocks, some cut off from the beach by the main road, over which there is a pedestrian bridge. The resort is growing, but it is still the smallest and quietest of the big three and caters mainly for retired couples and families with young children, although it is also very popular with windsurfers. There is a fairly small, safe beach, a number of watersports facilities and some attractive apartments, most set in gardens among palms and poinsettia, and with their own swimming pools.

The Count's Vision

The Conde del Castillo de la Vega Grande de Guadelupe, an aristocrat with a pedigree as long as his name, had a family home in Telde, in a building that is now the town hall. He also had large tracts of unused and seemingly useless land in the barren south of the island. Nobody lived there, nothing would grow there and the land was a liability. In the early 1960s, however, as the tourist boom swept through mainland Spain, the Count came up with a scheme that would change the face and the economy of Gran Canaria. Out of the desert he constructed what are now the resorts of San Agustín, Playa del Inglés and Maspalomas. Tour companies, quick to spot a potential gold mine, soon moved building contractors in. Where else would you find streets named after tour operators as you do in Maspalomas? Within two decades the south of Gran Canaria had developed into a huge holiday complex, attracting visitors from northern Europe, mainly on all-inclusive package holidays, providing employment for islanders and further enriching the man who masterminded the project.

Following the paved promenade to the west of the resort you will come to **Playa de las Burras**, known locally as Playa Chica – the little beach – around which cluster a villa complex, a well-stocked supermarket and a small shopping centre.

Hotel Faro

Playa del Inglés

You can walk along the promenade from San Agustín to **Playa del Inglés**. As you go, you will notice that the sand becomes more golden, the apartment blocks get taller and visitors' clothing grows scantier. Approach direct from the motorway and you will find yourself suddenly in a grid of wide streets lined with large hotels, restaurants, car-hire outlets and retail opportunities, and peopled by a relentless march of hot tourists carrying beach gear.

Playa del Inglés is a big place, but there is a good bus service, taxis are cheap and reliable, and hotels further from the beach provide frequent free buses. There are several huge commercial centres, the largest being the oddly-named **Yumbo Centre**, in which you will find the main tourist information office, presided over by efficient, multilingual staff. Among the numerous bars and clubs in the centre are quite a few that cater to the gay community.

The beach is the main event, of course. The **Paseo Costa Canaria** is an attractive pedestrian promenade, lined with smart villa complexes and bright with tropical blooms, that runs the length of it, from Playa de las Burras to the point where the Maspalomas dunes begin. On the sands below, sun

The dunes of Maspalomas offer a wonderful sense of freedom

loungers and beach umbrellas are arranged in serried ranks, and the more energetic visitors try their hand at waterskiing, windsurfing and parasailing.

Descend via stairs or escalators to the **Paseo Marítimo**. Protected by awnings from the heat of the sun, this is a 2-km (1¼-mile) stretch of fast food outlets, amusement arcades, Irish pubs and German beer kellers with extended Happy Hours, tattoo parlours, Internet cafés and shops selling sandals, sarongs and sun hats.

Maspalomas

Maspalomas is divided from Playa del Inglés by a spectacular stretch of **dunes**, covering an area of 4 sq km (1½ sq miles), that in 1994 were designated a nature reserve in order to preserve the ecosystem. The contrast between these pristine mountains of sand and the commercialism of the resort is quite remarkable. You can walk over the dunes if you protect your feet from the hot sand, and camel safaris are organised, although environmentalists oppose them. Adjoining the dunes, a golf course forms another barrier between the neighbourhoods, but inland the two resorts almost merge into each other, although their style is distinctive. Accommodation in Maspalomas is in smart hotels, bungalows or low-rise apartment complexes set in large, lush gardens, for this is altogether a more upmarket resort.

The main road, the Carretera General a Las Palmas, swoops past the **Ocean Park** waterpark (open daily 10am–6pm; admission fee) all the way round the sprawling Maspalomas development to **El Faro**, the lighthouse. From here a palm-lined *paseo* leads to the area known as **El Oasis**, a place of ultra-smart hotels beside **La Charca** *(see panel)*. You can drive back up the Avenida Oceania that parallels the Barranco de Maspalomas, a long, broad, palm-fringed riverbed that runs straight through the middle of the *urbanización*.

To the west of the lighthouse, in a sheltered bay, lies the luxury resort of **Las Meloneras**, with everything for the discerning visitor; while further inland **Sonnenland** is a relatively recent and not very appealing tourist complex.

> **La Charca, part of the Maspalomas nature reserve, is a little lagoon to which migratory and breeding birds, frightened away by human activity, are being encouraged to return. Moorhens, herons and kestrels have ventured back to its reed beds and ospreys are occasionally seen.**

Inland Excursions

When the swimming pool loses its sparkle and the beach becomes a bore, there are plenty of excursions to be made to attractions just a little way inland. A car isn't necessary because there are regular bus services from convenient stops. **Mundo Aborigen**, a well-structured re-creation of life in a Guanche settlement, and the **Camel Safari Park** are both a few kilometres up the road to Fataga, while **Palmitos Park**, a big ornithological park with an aquarium, butterfly house and botanic garden is on the road inland from Maspalomas. **Sioux City**, a Wild West theme park, lies in the Cañón del Águila, just east of San Agustín, but buses pick up passengers from all the resorts. *(For more details on all these attractions see What to Do, pages 88–9.)*

Puerto Rico

The first community west of Maspalomas is **Pasito Blanco**, a little port and resort mainly of interest to sailing enthusiasts *(see page 83)*. Next is **Arguiniguín**, which has seen quite a bit of development in recent years, but is still a working fishing port and community and therefore rather pleasant after so much artificiality. The elderly men playing draughts in the Centro Socio Cultural don't seem bothered by the comings and goings of the tourists who disembark from cruise ships or pleasure craft. Apartment blocks of the new holiday complex of **Patalavaca** loom around the cliffs, and shortly after that you arrive at **Puerto Rico**.

Puerto Rico is a family-oriented resort

If you want to expand and develop a pleasant little bay surrounded by sheer cliffs, you can build a landscaped promenade and a few attractive seaside villas, but after that the only way to go is up. That is what the entrepreneurs of Puerto Rico did when the resort was con-

Welcoming water in Puerto Rico

ceived in the 1970s and the result is a wall of apartment blocks rising to the top of the hills, like tiers of seats in a giant amphitheatre. Below, space is at a premium, and sun beds are even lined up along the length of a jetty. The clean little beach is family-oriented – the families are predominantly English – and when kids tire of the sand there is **Aquapark** (open daily 10am–6pm; admission fee), with a huge water slide among its delights.

Puerto Rico has a serious reputation as a sailing centre and members of its club have won five Olympic medals. Deep-sea fishermen, not to be outdone, have claimed nearly three dozen world records in their sport. Naturally, then, the **Puerto Deportivo** caters for visiting fishing and water sports enthusiasts and for those who just like being on the water. There are diving schools and sailing schools, deep-sea fishing trips, 'dolphin search' trips in glass-bottomed catamarans, or simple pleasure trips that run up and down the coast.

Puerto de Mogán

Passing yet another new development, the Playa de los Amadores, the road to Puerto de Mogán winds past some extraordinary rock formations and two deep gorges, the Barranco de Tauro and the Barranco del Taurito, each with a corresponding beach. Built round a complex of sea-water canals with delicately arched bridges, **Puerto de Mogán** is almost impossibly pretty. The windows and flat roofs of its twostorey houses are outlined in shades of blue, green and ochre, the walls smothered with multicoloured bougainvillaea and trailing geraniums.

There are two ports here, the sensible, working one that was once the town's *raison d'être* and from which a fishing fleet still operates; and the **Puerto Deportivo**, where luxurious yachts bob in the water. This leisure port is lined with cafés and restaurants, all offering wonderful views and similar fish and seafood menus. The buildings that line the streets behind the harbour are equally picturesque and some of them house yet more restaurants and a smattering of above-average gift shops.

Submarine Adventure offers trips in a yellow submarine *(see page 89)* and pleasure boats ply back and forth between here, Puerto Rico and Arguiniguín, but most visitors are content simply to wander the streets and sit in the cafés. Those with children make for the small beach to the east of the port, which is being 'sandscaped' and extended.

On Friday a huge market lines the fishermen's quay,

> The Fiestas del Carmen, celebrating the patron saint of fishermen, take place throughout July in Arguiniguín and Puerto de Mogán. Celebrations include firework displays, concerts and dances and culminate in a maritime procession, led by a decorated boat carrying the statue of the Virgin.

There's still a fishing fleet in Puerto de Mogán

selling African carvings, bead jewellery, aromatherapy oils, island cheeses, exotic local fruits, beach sarongs and imitation Raybans. Busloads of tourists arrive from the neighbouring resorts around 10.30am and are whisked away with their purchases in the afternoon.

Mogán

The road inland wends its way up the fertile, fruit-producing *barranco* to Mogán. In season, you may be able to buy ripe papaya, mangoes and avocados by the roadside. Just before the town, a windmill stands sentinel by the road in the tiny hamlet of El Molino de Viento – which means windmill. Surrounded by jagged mountains, **Mogán** is a sleepy little place with a picture-postcard church dedicated to San Antonio, colourful, well-watered gardens in the central plaza and towering palms outside the town hall. If you come in high season, when visitors drive up from the coast in hired jeeps, there will be a buzz of activity on the streets and in a couple of rather good restaurants. Otherwise, the sound of goats bleating in the *barranco* may be the only noise you hear.

GOING WEST

The west of Gran Canaria is for those who like a challenge. It is the area least visited by tourists; the roads are vertiginous and villages few and far between. But there are stunning rock formations and mountain landscapes, marvellous views and a chance to experience a region that feels quite remote although it's only a few hours' drive from Las Palmas.

The Mountain Route

The road from Mogán twists and turns on its way to San Nicolás de Tolentino, cutting through rocks of red, grey and gold and passing isolated houses where convolvulus clings

A sinuous road snakes through the bare hills

tenaciously to crumbling walls. To your right soar the Montaña de Sándara, the Montaña de las Monjas, and the peak of Inagua, all over 1,400m (4,600ft) high. To the left, three deep gorges run down to the sea. The first is the **Barranco de Veneguera**, where a track – which should only be attempted in a four-wheel-drive vehicle – leads 10km (6 miles) through banana

Vivid rock colours at the Fuente de los Azulejos

plantations to a lovely, unspoiled beach. After years of protests environmentalists have won a battle to prevent the valley being developed for tourism, and in 2003 it was incorporated into the Parque Rural del Nublo.

The road running through the next gorge, the **Barranco de Tasarte**, is a bit better, and also culminates in a pretty beach. From the third gully, the **Barranco de Tasártico**, there is a long, arduous hike through the **Reserva Natural Especial de Güi-Güi**, where 3,000 hectares (7,400 acres) of land have been put under a protection order to safeguard the vegetation clinging to the rocks. Those who can go the distance will be rewarded with an idyllic little beach.

Just past the Tasarte turning, to the right of the road, is **La Fuente de los Azulejos**, where oxidisation has turned the rocks bright green. Opposite, a roadside bar sells fresh papaya juice to drink and aloe vera to ease sunburn.

San Nicolás de Tolentino

As the road begins to straighten, you come to the village of **Tocodomán**, and **Cactualdea** (open daily 10am–6pm;

admission fee). This 'Cactus Village' has more varieties of cacti than you knew existed, all well-labelled and set among palms and dragon trees. There's also a replica Guanche cave, a restaurant serving typical Canarian dishes, wine tasting opportunities and, of course, a gift shop.

You won't be able to miss the fact that swathes of land here are covered in plastic. Beneath the plastic grow tomatoes, the crop that is the mainstay of the region and of its only proper town, **San Nicolás de Tolentino** (officially known as La Aldea de San Nicolás). The town doesn't have a lot going for it, but it's a friendly place that tries hard to attract visi-

> **The tomato industry is not as prosperous as it once was, as it now faces stiff competition from Moroccan growers. Despite this, the region still exports some 100,000kg (220,000lbs) of early varieties per annum.**

tors. A helpful little tourist office on the right as you enter town offers informative leaflets and has some *artesanía* items for sale, the woven textiles showing distinct Latin American influences. The town used to be a craft centre but these days weaving and pottery are hobbies rather than a way of making a living. There is one plain, modern hotel and a *pensión* with a restaurant offering 'home style cooking'.

Puerto de la Aldea

Some 3km (2 miles) down the road is **Puerto de la Aldea** – which simply means the Port of the Village. The port is tiny, but there seems to be enough fish brought in to keep several restaurants flourishing. Beside a long pebbly beach a smartly tiled promenade has just been completed. Parallel to it runs a shady garden with stone picnic tables set beneath pine trees.

At the far end lies **El Charco** (The Lagoon), a fairly non-descript pond for most of the year but the site, every 11 September, of the Fiesta del Charco, when local people attempt to catch fish with their bare hands and to duck each other in the water. The origins of this strange custom are uncertain, but it is believed to date from pre-Hispanic times. *Lucha canaria* (wrestling) matches and stick-fighting competitions are an integral part of the festival.

An aboriginal settlement close by, **Los Caserones**, has yielded a great many archaeological finds, including the bones of a Verdino dog, the emblem of the Canary Islands. The remains of the settlement can be seen on a small hill.

The Coastal Road

The journey up the coast is one that demands concentration. The road winds past bare rock on one side and steep cliffs, plunging straight into the ocean, on the other. Fortunately, two *miradors* (viewpoints) have been created at points of

Admiring the stunning views from the Mirador del Balcón

particular beauty, so drivers can stop to admire the views. The first is the **Mirador del Balcón**, the second the **Andén Verde**. To the north the craggy coastline runs up to the Punto de Góngora; straight ahead, across miles of dark blue sea, lies Tenerife, crowned with the peak of El Teide, at 3,718m (11,898ft) the highest mountain in Spain.

Puerto de las Nieves

You pass only one village along the way, El Risco, and there are still many curves to go before you arrive at **Puerto de las Nieves** (The Harbour of the Snows). The name derives not from any freak snowfall but from Nuestra Señora de las Nieves, the Madonna of the Snows, patron saint of the local fishermen. Her tiny chapel, known as the **Ermita de las Nieves**, houses a real treasure, a 16th-century Flemish triptych attributed to Joos van Cleve, depicting the Virgin and Child

Puerto de las Nieves is a quiet and pretty place

flanked by saints Francis and Antony. The ribbed and decorated wooden ceiling above the choir is said to be *mudéjar*, the architecture of the Moors who remained in Spain after the reconquest in the 11th century.

The church does not have regular opening hours but the key is kept by a Señor Antonio, who can often be found in a neighbouring bar (ask in a local shop or restaurant). However, Señor Antonio is very old indeed and a new key holder may be sought in the near future.

The Ermita de las Nieves houses a great treasure

The Harbour

In the harbour fishing boats bob gently beside a new jetty, where wooden decking has been laid down for the benefit of sunbathers. A number of restaurants line the quay, serving excellent fish at reasonable prices *(see page 138)*. They get very busy at weekends, when people from Las Palmas come for lunch. Otherwise, the main bursts of activity are the arrivals and departures six times a day of the ferries to Santa Cruz de Tenerife, run by the Fred Olsen line (a free bus service from Las Palmas connects with the port).

A great deal of investment has gone into the village in recent years, in an attempt to compensate for the declining fishing industry. A large new hotel has been built close to the remains of a Guanche cemetery, but on the whole the development has been sympathetic. A new promenade, called the Paseo de los Poetas, has been constructed, lined with blue and white restaurants. Some low-rise apartment blocks and villas have sprung up in the streets behind it, blending quite nicely with the single-storey fishermen's cottages.

At the southern end of the village, at the foot of the dramatic coastline you have just negotiated, the **Dedo de Dios** (Finger of God), is a slender pinnacle of rock rising from the sea. On the beach below is a restaurant named after it.

Agaete

Return to the main road and almost immediately you are in **Agaete**, where a number of the houses have carved wooden balconies. In the Plaza de la Constitución, as you enter the town, stands the imposing, 19th-century Iglesia de la Concepción, and nearby, off Calle Huertas, the **Huerto de las Flores** (open Mon–Fri 9am–2pm; free) is a small botanical garden with some rare trees.

The town stands at the entrance to the dramatic **Barranco de Agaete**, a green and fertile gorge that is signposted simply as **El Valle** (The Valley). It's a lovely place to drive or walk. Avocados, oranges, lemons and mangoes grow on terraces clinging to the steep sides of the valley. Lofty Canary

---

Bringing Down the Branches

Puerto de las Nieves and Agaete are renowned for a festival known as Bajada de las Ramas (Bringing Down the Branches), celebrated with great enthusiasm on 4–5 August each year. Residents of the two communities gather branches from the hillsides and carry them down to the harbour, where they whip the waves with them before laying them at the feet of the Virgin of the Snows. Although this provides a religious context, the ritual has pagan origins, and, like many festivals, was intended to bring both rain and fertility. It's a high-spirited occasion, with lots of music and dancing, feasting and frolicking, and people come from all over the island to take part.

palms, solitary agaves and prickly pears gradually give way, on the upper slopes, to the Canary pine.

The road goes only as far as the little village of Los Berrazales. Shortly before the end, smothered in geraniums, stands the atmospheric old Princess Guayarmina hotel *(see page 127)*.

THE NORTH

There are some 700 hectares (1,730 acres) of protected land in the north of the island, the best known area

Bringing down the Branches at Agaete's annual festival

being the **Reserva Natural de los Tilos de Moya**. Away from these reserves, the landscape is fairly barren, for the forests of bay laurel *(Laurus canariensis)* that once covered it in green were cut down in the 16th century to provide fuel for the sugar industry. Yet more land was cleared to make way for bananas, introduced as a monocrop by the English more than three centuries later. The principal crop today is still bananas, many of which are grown in mammoth plastic tunnels.

In marked contrast to the sparsely populated west coast, this small area encompasses half a dozen towns: Gáldar, Guía, Moya, Arucas, Firgas and Teror. All are worth visiting and all involve circuitous, winding roads. It is often easier to return to the main coastal road between towns, rather than take what looks like the shortest route. Only a short stretch of new motorway from Las Palmas has been completed so far but the straight coast road is quite adequate.

Gáldar

The hill on which **Gáldar** is set resembles an extinct volcano, with the town clustered at its feet. It's only about 8km (5 miles) between Agaete and Gáldar, but the pace of life seems to shift up a notch. Park as soon as you find a space because traffic is heavy and the one-way streets are confusing.

Gáldar is known as the Ciudad de los Guanartemes (City of Rulers), as it was the seat of Tenesor Semidan, one of the island's two Guanche chiefs. The town is proud of its heritage and many of the streets and squares have Guanche names. Post-conquest Gáldar was founded in 1484 and was the capital of Gran Canaria before Las Palmas.

The **Iglesia de Santiago de los Caballeros**, in a shady square, was built on the spot where Semidan's palace supposedly stood. Begun in 1778, it was the first neoclassical building on the island. It houses a number of statues attributed to José Luján Pérez (1756–1815), who was born nearby in Santa María de Guía. The Ayuntamiento (Town Hall), in the same square, has a huge dragon tree in its courtyard. Planted in 1718, it is said to be the oldest in the archipelago.

The Iglesia de Santiago de los Caballeros in Gáldar

Around the corner in Calle Tagoror is Ca' Juancrí, a good old-fashioned bar with a panelled interior, tango music on tape and a wide variety of tapas.

Despite local feelings of pride, the Patrimonio Histórico – the government department in charge of cultural affairs – has been somewhat slow to exploit Gáldar's legacy. The **Cueva Pintada** (Painted Cave), in the town centre, decorated with coloured geometric patterns, is an important Guanche relic, but it has been closed for renovation for many years. It is due to reopen in 2004. There's a replica of the cave in the Museo Canario in Las Palmas *(see page 31)*. Another important archaeological

At the eastern entrance to Gáldar a sculpture represents three Guanche princesses. Another sculpture in the town depicts Tenesor Semidan, the chieftain who reluctantly accepted baptism and collaborated with the Spanish.

site, reached by a lane running through banana plantations towards the coast, is the **Poblado y Necrópolo de la Guancha**, where numerous mummies were found. This, too, has been closed for several years and is currently only open to groups, by prior arrangement (tel: 928 219 421 for details).

Sardina

From the roundabout to the west of Gáldar (the same way you came in), the main road west leads to **Sardina**, a tiny resort on a small beach, popular with snorkellers and protected by dark, volcanic rocks. A harbourside restaurant offers satisfying fish dishes and a view of the beach. Sardina is pretty quiet during the week but attracts people from Gáldar and Las Palmas at weekends. North of the village a lighthouse stands on the windy Punta de Sardina.

Santa María de Guía

The next town, going east from Gáldar at the same roundabout, is little **Santa María de Guía**, usually just known as Guía, famous for its *queso de flor*. This is a cheese made from sheep and cows' milk, mixed with the juice of cardoon thistle flowers. Strange as it may sound, it tastes very good and has won prizes. You can try some in a cavernous shop

The pre-Hispanic Cenobio de Valerón is an intriguing place

(Calle Marqués de Muni 34) belonging to the ebullient Santiago Gil Romero, whose family have been selling it here for three generations. A traditional cheese festival is held here on May Day *(see page 94)* and on nearby Montaña Alta on the following Sunday.

There are some attractive, brightly painted houses in Guía's Casco Histórico, and an imposing, two-towered church in the Plaza Grande (not very big, despite its name) where a market is held every Tuesday morning.

Cenobio de Valerón

Take the main road now for Moya, but turn off first where you see signs to the **Cenobio de Valerón** (open Wed–Sun 10am–5pm; admission fee). *Cenobio* means convent and this complex of about 300 caves, hollowed out of the soft, volcanic rock, was once believed to have been a place where *harimagüadas* – young virgins – were detained in order to protect their purity until they married. However, it is now widely accepted that the caves were grain stores, which were easily defensible because of their isolated position.

Moya

The GC-75, the next turning off the main road, winds up hill to the friendly, sleepy, little town of **Moya**. There's a helpful tourist office (open daily), and an impressive church, **Nuestra Señora de Candelaria**, begun in the 16th century but with many later additions. It is home to some interesting pieces of sculpture, including a 15th-century cedar wood figure of the Virgin of Candelaria, and several works by Luján Pérez, but unfortunately it is often closed except when early evening services are in progress.

Moya is the birthplace of the island's best-loved poet, Tomás Morales (1885–1921) and his home, the **Casa-Museo Morales** (open Mon–Fri 9am–8pm, Sat 10am–2pm, 5–8pm, Sun 10am–2pm; free) stands in the square opposite the church. It's an intimate little place – particularly The Poet's Room – with first editions of Morales' work, his Remington typewriter and lots of photos, paintings and poems on the walls. The bronze statue of the poet outside was erected in 1999. Morales is one of the poets after whom the Paseo de los Poetas in Puerto de las Nieves was named. The other two are his contemporaries, Alonso Quesada and Saulo Torón.

A portrait of Morales in the museum dedicated to him

From the top of the town a road leads past neatly cultivated vegetable gardens on the valley slopes to **Los Tilos de Moya**, a 91-hectare (225-acre) nature reserve – although it is laurels not *tilos* (limes) that are being protected. Swathes of them once covered the island but few remain, and the protection order has been placed in an attempt to re-establish them.

Arucas

Unless you want to visit the centre of the island, retrace your route to the main road and at Bañaderos, take the turning to **Arucas**. As you enter the town, the **Parque Municipal** is on your left, a shady spot full of exotic trees and plants. You will soon get pulled into the busy one-way system, so park as soon as possible and explore the **Casco Histórico** on foot. The huge lava-stone church of **San Juan Bautista** (open daily 9.30am–12.30pm, 4.30–7.15pm; free), begun in 1909, is said to owe its inspiration to Antoni Gaudí's Sagrada

A huge, lava-stone church dominates the town of Arucas

Família in Barcelona, and there are some similar Modernista flourishes. Inside, it is more conventionally neo-Gothic, and has three splendid rose windows.

In the nearby Calle León y Castillo a statue of the poet Domingo Rivero, book in hand, stands in front of a giant cactus outside the Casa de Cultura. Rivero, great-uncle of Tomás Morales, was born here in 1852. Inside, leading off a pleasant courtyard with a dragon tree, are much-frequented reading rooms for adults and children.

One of the reasons traffic is heavy in Arucas is that tourists' vehicles must wend their way through the old town to reach the nearby **Montaña de Arucas**. This is where the Guanche leader, Doramas, was killed in single-handed combat by Pedro de Vera in 1480. His followers are said to have leapt to their deaths in the *barranco* rather than surrender. Today, there's an observation point offering great views.

Firgas and the Finca de Osorio

From Arucas there are two routes to Teror. The longer one, on the GC-300, will take you via the pleasant little town of **Firgas**, where a man-made waterfall cascades 30m (90ft) down shallow steps in the centre of a pedestrianised street. Firgas is known for its water. There's a natural spring just south of the town and the remarkably tasty product is bottled and sold all over the island.

The more direct route is on the GC-43. This one will take you past the **Finca de Osorio** (tel: 928 630 090; open Sat–Sun 9am–5pm; other times by appointment; free). This rural mansion is used as an *Aula de la Naturaleza* – a place where school groups and college students come, some on residential courses, to learn about conservation, wildlife and agriculture. The formal gardens are rich with roses and magnolias and the forested land around the house is a favourite picnic spot for local families.

Teror

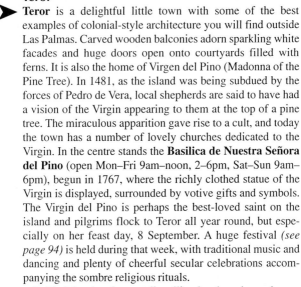

Teror is a delightful little town with some of the best examples of colonial-style architecture you will find outside Las Palmas. Carved wooden balconies adorn sparkling white facades and huge doors open onto courtyards filled with ferns. It is also the home of Virgen del Pino (Madonna of the Pine Tree). In 1481, as the island was being subdued by the forces of Pedro de Vera, local shepherds are said to have had a vision of the Virgin appearing to them at the top of a pine tree. The miraculous apparition gave rise to a cult, and today the town has a number of lovely churches dedicated to the Virgin. In the centre stands the **Basilica de Nuestra Señora del Pino** (open Mon–Fri 9am–noon, 2–6pm, Sat–Sun 9am–6pm), begun in 1767, where the richly clothed statue of the Virgin is displayed, surrounded by votive gifts and symbols. The Virgin del Pino is perhaps the best-loved saint on the island and pilgrims flock to Teror all year round, but especially on her feast day, 8 September. A huge festival *(see page 94)* is held during that week, with traditional music and dancing and plenty of cheerful secular celebrations accompanying the sombre religious rituals.

Behind the church are stalls selling local produce – homemade bread, cheese and vegetables – as well as religious items. In front stands the Palacio Episcopal (Bishop's Palace), which now houses a cultural centre. On the right-hand side of the basilica, is the **Museo de los Patrones de la Virgen del Pino** (open Mon–Thur and Sat 11.30am–7pm, Sun 10.30am–2pm; admission fee) in a beautiful building, set around a courtyard and furnished in the style of a noble, 17th-centu-

A sensible sign in the Basilica de Nuestra Señora del Pino reads: 'Although the Virgin is grateful for your gifts and candles she would rather you gave your money to the poor.'

The Plaza Teresa de Bolívar is a peaceful spot

ry home. It belongs, as it always has, to the Manrique de Lara family, who still spend the festival week here. At the back of the house are an old bakery and a stable block, where Don Manrique's polished 1951 Triumph shares space with sedan chairs, carts and carriages.

There is a smaller square close by, the **Plaza Teresa de Bolívar**, with a stone fountain in the centre. It is named after the first wife of Simón de Bolívar, the man who led the liberation of many of the Spanish colonies in South America in the 19th century. Her family came from Teror; his from Tenerife. The couple met in Venezuela, but Teresa died less than a year after they were married.

The centre of Teror is closed to traffic, so you can wander through the cobbled alleys and little squares and drink in the atmosphere without being disturbed by noise or fumes. If you come on Sunday morning you will also be able to enjoy the busy, and very local, market.

THE CENTRAL PEAKS

In order to appreciate the age and majesty of the planet and the relative insignificance of human beings, all you need is a trip to the central peaks of Gran Canaria. Over millions of years volcanic eruptions, fierce winds and driving rain have moulded and sculpted the rocks into strange shapes, and erosion has also created deep *barrancos* (gorges) that radiate out from the centre and descend to the coast, their fertile soil supporting lush vegetation.

The highest peaks are Pico de las Nieves (Peak of the Snows) at 1,949m (6,394ft), followed by Roque Nublo (Rock of Clouds), at 1,803m (5,915ft), and Roque Bentaiga (1,412m/ 4,632ft). Below them, mountain villages cling to the rock and narrow terraces are cultivated wherever possible. Much of the central area is protected as part of the Parque Rural del

The central peaks of Gran Canaria are an awe-inspiring sight

Nublo; while the land to the west of Artenara forms the Parque Natural de Tamadaba. While the mountains obviously have a huge appeal for climbers and serious walkers, there are many relatively short and easy walks that can be made amid stunning scenery, some of them on the *caminos reales (see panel on page 79)*, others on newer paths.

The central region can be reached quite easily from most parts of the island: direct from Las Palmas; from the northern towns of Arucas and Moya; from Agüimes in the east; or from the southern resorts, via the Barranco de Fataga. Only from the wild west coast, where tracks either peter out altogether or challenge the toughest vehicles and most confident drivers, are the peaks inaccessible.

If you're approaching from Las Palmas you can take the Santa Brígida road through **Vega San Mateo** (usually known simply as San Mateo) and up the tortuous road to Tejeda, where bus drivers sound their horns as they approach every sharp bend. Or you could avoid the stress and take bus No. 303, changing at Vega San Mateo where you can have a peek at the rural life museum (free) in **Hotel La Cantonera** in Avenida Tinamar, almost opposite the bus station. As the road climbs upwards, the lush vegetation changes. If you go in spring or early summer you will notice rampaging nasturtiums, blossoming lavender bushes and neat orange groves on the first part of the journey. Next come the prickly pear cactus *(Opuntia ficus indica)* eucalyptus trees and century plants *(Agave),* before the entire hillside turns yellow with broom and, close to the top, the pines and holm oaks begin.

Cruz de Tejeda

The top of the pass, at 1,580m (5,184ft), is marked by a sombre, stone crucifix, the **Cruz de Tejeda**. Surrounded by towering peaks, this is a hive of commercial activity, with two bustling restaurants (one, El Refugio, is also a hotel), a shop specialising in aniseed-flavoured cakes, and a row of stalls selling embroidered tablecloths, ponchos, beach towels, dried fruit and stuffed camels. There's also a man offering donkey rides to children.

Behind the cross, stands a *parador*, the Hostería de Cruz de Tejeda, designed in the 1930s by Néstor Martín-Fernández de la Torre *(see page 32)*. If open, it would be a splendid place to stay, but renovation and extension work has been going on for some time, and it is uncertain when it will be completed. To find out if it has re-opened at the time of your visit, ask the tourist office in Las Palmas (tel: 928 219 600).

The view is dominated by the impressive, pointing finger of **Roque Nublo**, which will have been visible for some time. Depending on the weather and the time of day, the huge monolith appears to change colour and is not hard to understand why the Guanches revered this as a holy place. A *camino real (see page 79)* leads from Cruz de Tejeda to Roque Nublo, but there is a shorter walk from Ayacata *(see page 77)*. On a clear morning especially, there is a breathtaking view across the entire island. Away in the distance, Tenerife's Mt Teide, snow-capped for much of the year, seems to rise straight out of the sea.

Taking a break in the sun at the Cruz de Tejeda

Artenara

There is a difficult but beautiful drive from Tejeda to **Artenara**, which, at an altitude of 1,270m (4,167ft), is the highest village on the island. It also one of the oldest, pre-dating the Spanish conquest, and Artenara is its

Guanche name. Many of the houses in the village are built into the solid rock, although some of them, with their painted facades, look like ordinary houses, and most have modern amenities. There is a cave church, **La Ermita de la Cuevita**, identified only by a bell above the door. It houses the *Virgen de la Cuevita*, whose festival is celebrated at the end of August. The Iglesia de San Matías is a more conventional church.

Mesón La Silla is on most visitors' itineraries, a cave restaurant entered via a long tunnel. It has a sunny terrace with magnificent

The sombre stone cross *(cruz)* that marks Tejeda

views of Roque Bentaiga and Roque Nublo and the substantial island dishes – *ropa vieja, papas arrugadas* and grilled meats – are good value.

Pinar de Tamadaba

From Artenara, a road leads around the **Pinar de Tamadaba**, 8 sq km (3 sq miles) of protected forest within a much larger nature park, where Canary pines *(Pinus canariensis)* grow to enormous heights, untroubled by pollution – some reach almost 60m (190ft). Forest fires occur periodically, but the pine is capable of rapid regeneration. There are footpaths through the forest but great care must be taken not to cause fires or in any way damage the environment. The road does not lead beyond the *pinar*, so you have to return the way you came.

Barranco de Fataga

If approaching the central peaks from the south, you should take the Fataga road from Playa del Inglés. This leads through the beautiful **Barranco de Fataga**, where burnished walls of rock are reminiscent of canyons in the American West. After an easy start, the bends in the road become tighter and the valley is greener. Palm trees line the roadside and tropical fruits are cultivated on the valley floor. Passing Mundo Aborigen and the Camel Safari Park *(see page 88)* you soon arrive in the village of **Fataga**, perched precipitously on a rock jutting out into the gorge. There's a nice church and several cheerful restaurants

A camel safari through the Barranco de Fataga

catering to visitors on jeep safaris from the coast, some of them offering barbecues and live music.

The road winds towards **San Bartolomé de Tirajana**, an historic little town and the administrative centre of a region that includes Maspalomas and Playa del Inglés. The town's main source of income is the production of fruit, especially cherries. The Ayuntamiento (Town Hall) has an attractive inner courtyard, and there are two churches – the neoclassical San Bartolomé, outside which a market is held on Sunday morning, and Santiago el Apóstol. The festival of Santiago (St James) is a major event on 25 July. You may want to stop at the petrol station here for fuel, as garages are few and far between in the mountains.

> The mountain regions specialise in liqueurs. *Guindilla* is a cherry liqueur made in San Bartolomé and takes its name from the Spanish word for morello cherries – *guindas. Mejunje* is a sweet concoction of rum, honey and lemon that was traditionally served to priests when they visited their parishioners.

Pico de las Nieves and Roque Bentaiga

Following signs to Tejeda you will reach the little village of **Ayacata**, from where there is a popular and not too demanding walk to **Roque Nublo**, which takes about 40 minutes each way. It passes another, smaller, rock figure known as El Fraile (The Monk). If you look carefully you may (just) see a resemblance to a praying monk.

Off to the right a road wriggles round a reservoir, the Presa de los Hornos. Not far away is the **Centro de Interpretación Degollada de Bercerra** (open daily 10am–5pm; free), an information centre with a *mirador* offering panoramic views. Looming above is the **Pico de las Nieves**, the highest peak on the island, crowned by a radar station and TV transmitter. The summit is not accessible as it is used as a military base, but there is a lookout point not far below.

The road to the west from Ayacata, signposted to Bentaiga, is asphalted at first but soon becomes a gravel track. After Roque Nublo, **Roque Bentaiga** is the most spectacular monolith in the range. In 1483 it was the site of a fierce battle in which the Spaniards, led by Pedro de Vera, defeated the Guanches. A Guanche refuge, called the Cueva del Rey (King's Cave), lies at the foot of the outcrop. It is well worth stopping at the **Centro de Interpretación** (open daily 11am–5pm; admission fee) for background information. From here, those with enough energy can scramble the last stretch up to the peak.

A quiet corner in the village of Santa Lúcia

Fortaleza Grande and Santa Lucía

An alternative way to approach the central peaks is from the east, from Agüimes, via Santa Lucía on the GC-550 or from the Cruce de Sardina exit off the motorway (GC-65). It almost goes without saying that these are winding roads with sharp bends, but the scenery is spectacular, with prickly pears, euphorbia and olive trees gradually losing ground to bare, reddish rock.

Off to the left of the GC-65 you will see **Fortaleza Grande**, a rock uncannily shaped like a castle, which was one of the last refuges of the Guanches. Some of those who survived the defeat at Roque Bentaiga obeyed the command of their leader, Tenesor Semidan, to surrender; others, it is said, threw themselves from these cliffs.

Surrounded by pines, **Santa Lucía** is a beautiful little village with blindingly-white houses, bougainvillaea tumbling over walls, and an imposing domed church with a double bell-tower. Most visitors stop at Restaurant Hao *(see page 139)* for grilled meat and *papas arrugadas,* served at long wooden benches. There's a children's playground and a small museum, the **Museo Castillo de la Fortaleza** (open daily 9am–5pm; admission fee) where Guanche artefacts, agricultural tools and a Roman amphora are displayed.

A final way to approach the peaks is via Moya or Arucas in the north *(see pages 67 and 68)*. The road from Arucas is better, but the Moya route goes past the Pinos de Gáldar pine forest. Both lead – circuitously, of course – to Cruz de Tejeda.

Caminos Reales

A series of ancient paths known as *caminos reales* – royal paths – have been restored and opened up to walkers as part of an attempt to promote conservation-conscious tourism and *senderismo* – hiking. These old tracks, once the only means of getting around the interior of Gran Canaria, centre on Cruz de Tejeda and radiate out to much of the island, from Maspalomas in the south to Agaete in the northwest. While some are demanding, others are relatively short and quite gentle. For more information, contact the Patronato de Turismo, Calle León y Castillo 17, Las Palmas (tel: 928 219 600), or go to the helpful government bookshop, the Librería del Cabildo Insular, Calle Cano 24, Las Palmas (tel: 928 381 539) for maps and books in English.

WHAT TO DO

SPORTS

The spectrum of sports and outdoor activities available on Gran Canaria runs from the extremely vigorous to the mildly energetic. While most of the activities take place on, in or under the water, there are many land-based pursuits, from hiking to horseriding and golf.

Windsurfing

Gran Canaria is considered one of the best places in the world for windsurfing – some say that only Hawaii beats it. It can be practised all along the coast running from Melenera in the east to Maspalomas in the south. **Playa de Vargas** near Arinaga is the venue for the annual PWA Wave Classic Grand Prix. Here and at nearby **Pozo Izquierdo**, strong winds are constant all year round and waves always high. A little further south, near San Agustín, winds are good in Bahía Feliz and Playa del Águila.

The two best windsurf schools, which offer beginners' and advanced courses, are **Club Mistral Canarias**, Urbanización Bahía Feliz, tel/fax: 928 157 158, e-mail: club_Mistral@infocanarias.com; and **F2 Surfcenter Dunkerbeck**. Plaza de Hibiscus 2, Playa del Águila, tel/fax: 928 762 958 (run by world champion Björn Dunkerbeck). Windsurfing conditions are also good on the Playa de las Canteras, Las Palmas and at Gáldar in the far northwest corner.

Surfing and Bodyboarding

The north of the island, between Las Palmas and Gáldar, is best for surfing and bodyboarding. Constant on-shore winds

Gran Canaria has excellent conditions for windsurfing

Sailing enthusiasts flock to the south coast

along this rocky coastline make ideal conditions for surfers and waves can be up to 5m (16ft) high. Conditions are also good around Arinaga, on the east coast and between Playa del Inglés and Maspalomas in the south.

Diving

There is a fascinating world beneath the waters off Gran Canaria and a number of excellent diving sites. In Las Palmas, where La Barra forms a giant aquarium, protected from the force of the waves, there is a wealth of underwater life to explore. On the east coast there is a diving centre at **Playa del Cabrón**, where the diversity of fish and vegetation is so great that the area has been designated a marine reserve. **Pasito Blanco**, on the south coast near **Puerto Rico**, is another good spot, with ideal conditions for underwater photography, and there are two wrecks in the waters off this coast to be explored by experienced divers. In the northwest, **Sardina** is a popular spot for night dives into rocky depths of 17m (52ft).

Reputable diving schools with qualified instructors include: **Buceo Canarias by Medusa Sub**, Calle Bernardo de la Torre 56–58, Las Palmas, tel: 928 262 786, <www.idecnet.com/medusasub>; **Centro Turístico de Submarinismo Sun Sub**, Hotel Buenaventura Playa, Plaza de Ansit s/n, Playa del Inglés, tel: 928 778 165, <www.sunsub.com>; **Top Diving**, Puerto Escala, Puerto Rico, tel: 928 560 609, <www.topdiving.net>. The latter has its own decompression chamber; **Playa del Cabrón** (tel: 699 721 584, <www.davyjonesdiving.com>).

Sailing

Gran Canaria is a sailors' dream, especially from April to October. Winds are reliably good and the climate is excellent. The main centres are Las Palmas and the south coast, specifically Pasito Blanco, Arguiniguín, Puerto Rico and Puerto de Mogán. The island attracts experienced sailors but is good for beginners too.

The annual Atlantic Rally for Cruisers (ARC) starts at the Muelle Deportivo in Las Palmas in Gran Canaria and makes the 2,700-nautical mile journey to St Lucia in the Caribbean. And members of Puerto Rico's sailing school have brought home five Olympic gold medals – three from Barcelona and two from Los Angeles.

To experience the sea while someone else does the work, take a trip in a glass bottom boat run by Líneas Salmon (tel: 649 919 383) or Líneas Blue Bird (tel: 928 224 151/629 989 633) between the ports of Arguiniguín, Puerto Rico and Puerto de Mogán. Or try the Super Cat from Puerto de Mogán (tel: 928 150 248) for a lazy day on a large sailing catamaran, with on-board barbecues.

Among many reliable sailing clubs and schools are: **Real Club Náutico**, Calle León y Castillo 308, Las Palmas, tel: 928 234 566, e-mail: nautica@nauticogcanaria.com; **Real Club Victoria**, Paseo de las Canteras 4, tel/fax: 928 460 630; **Escuela Deportiva Náutica Anfi del Mar**, Playa Barranco de la Vega, Mogán, tel/fax: 928 150 798, ext. 1556; and the **Club Regatas Suroeste Mogán**, Arguineguín, tel: 928 560 772. For information on lateen sailing, contact the **Federación de Vela Latina Canaria**, tel: 928 293 356, e-mail: vela-latina@tera.es.

Deep-sea Fishing

Gran Canaria is well-known for its game fishing and Pasito Blanco, Puerto Rico and Puerto de Mogán are the major centres. Puerto Rico's fishermen are the proud holders of 34 world records in deep-sea fishing, but this is a sport in which beginners can indulge, too, and it seems to bring out a bit of hidden Hemingway in many men. Several varieties of tuna and marlin as well as swordfish and, sometimes, sharks can

---

Lucha Canaria and Juego del Palo

Lucha canaria – Canary Islands wrestling – is the most popular traditional sport on the islands and can be seen at rural fiestas, in the Estadio López Socas in Las Palmas, and in Gáldar. Two teams of 12 wrestlers take it in turns to face a member of the opposing team in a sandy ring, with the aim of throwing the opponent to the ground. After a maximum of three rounds *(bregas)* the winner is the team that loses the fewest wrestlers. The game was practised in pre-Hispanic times, when it may have had more serious overtones.

Juego del Palo (stick fighting) is another ancient rural sport, also practised at fiestas. The object is to move the body as little as possible while attacking and fending off the blows of an opponent.

be found in these well-stocked waters. The deep-sea fishing season is roughly from May to September, but there is bottom-fishing available all year round.

A number of organisations offer fishing trips that include lunch and all the necessary equipment. Try **White Striker**, Puerto Rico, tel: 928 753 013, mobile: 689 744 967, with a knowledgeable skipper and an arrangement with a taverna on the jetty to cook the smaller fish you bring back. Tuna is sold direct to restaurants; marlin is collected by staff from a children's home in Las Palmas.

For general information, contact the **Club de Pesca de Altura**, Puerto Deportivo de Puerto Rico, tel: 928 561 141.

Walking

There's lots to do on land, and the most popular activity is hiking – *senderismo*. This is being promoted by the Cabildo Insular as a way of diversifying the tourist industry and encouraging visitors to explore the interior of the island. More than 66,000 hectares (164,000 acres) of land in Gran Canaria is under some kind of protection order. There are rural parks, nature reserves, fully protected reserves and natural monuments, and there is access to most of this land. A series of ancient paths, the *caminos reales*, or royal paths *(see page 79)*, once the only means of traversing much of the island, have been opened up for walkers. There are some challenging walks and climbs in the mountainous centre of the island, but there are many other less strenuous routes as well.

A guidebook to these paths can be purchased in the bookshop of the **Cabildo Insular de Gran Canario**, Calle Cano 24, Las Palmas. Or contact the Patronato de Turismo, León y Castillo 17, Las Palmas, tel: 928 219 600, fax: 928 219 601, <www.grancanaria.com>. They publish a series of leaflets, including maps, and although the information is in Spanish, basic details such as altitudes and length and duration of walks are clear. There is also a useful book called *Mountain Walks in Gran Canaria*, by Javier Martínez García (translated by Michal Adams), published by the Open Air Press, Dublin and available from the Cabildo Insular bookshop.

There are many other excellent walks though lush scenery in the island's *barrancos*. For general information on organised hikes, contact **Grupo Montañero Gran Canaria**, Calle 15 de Noviembre 6, Las Palmas, tel: 928 249 292. For group hikes with a knowledgeable guide in the Barranco de Guayadeque, contact **Caminos de Herradura**, Calle Drago 11, Agüimes, tel: 928 789 099, mobile: 616 871 671, e-mail: caminoherradura@terra.es.

Whether you are in a group or not, remember the basics: strong, comfortable shoes, sunblock, sun hat, sweater or jacket for lower temperatures in the mountains, and something to cover exposed shoulders in the sun. Take plenty of drinking water with you – it's easy to get dehydrated; and don't walk completely alone, in case of mishaps.

Golf

There are six golf courses in Gran Canaria, three in the north and three in the south. They include the **Real Club de Golf de Las Palmas**, Santa Brígida, tel: 928 350 104, e-mail: rcglp@step.es; 18 holes, par 71, the oldest club, founded by British expatriates in 1891; **Maspalomas Golf Club**, Avenida Neckermann s/n, tel: 928 762 581, e-mail: magolfsa @maspalomasgolf.net, <www.maspalomasgolf.net>; 18 holes, par 73, which has also been operating for some years; and the newer **Salobre Golf Club**, Autopista GC-1, Km53 between Maspalomas and Puerto de Mogán, tel: 928 010 103, e-mail: reservations@salobregolfresort.com; <www. salobregolfresort.com>; 18 holes, par 71; opened in 2000. For more information, visit the island's own golfing website, <www.grancanariagolf.org>.

Most golf courses welcome non-members

Horseriding

The **Real Club de Golf** at Santa Brígida (tel: 928 351 050) has a riding school. Riding lessons and trekking can be organised at **Rancho Park**, Playa del Inglés, on the road to Palmitos Park, tel: 928 766 874.

Flying, Parachuting and Sky Diving

If you want to try flying or parachuting, contact the **Escuela Canaria de Parapente**, Club Siroco, Las Palmas, tel: 928 267 520 (courses from beginners to advanced) or the **Aeroclub de Gran Canaria**, Carretera a Mogán 46, tel: 928 762 447. For sky diving – a 20-minute flight over the Maspalomas dunes and a jump in tandem with an instructor from 3,000m (9,840ft) – contact **Paraclub Gran Canaria**, tel: 928 157 000; or **Skydive Gran Canaria**, tel: 928 157 325, mobile: 670 808 102. Both operate from the far end of the Paseo Marítimo, where the dunes begin.

Jeep and Quad Safaris

Jeep safaris from Playa del Inglés to Fataga are popular. Some include a barbecue lunch in the price; some throw in a free video of your trip. Try **Discovery Jeep Safari**, tel: 928 775 188, mobile: 616 070 682.

Quad safaris are only for the young and daring. They go off-road on the route to Fataga along river beds and rocky tracks. Contact **Free Motion**, in the Sandy Beach Hotel, Avenida Aleréces Provisionales, Playa del Inglés, tel: 928 777 479, who also hire mountain bikes.

Jeep safaris are a good way to see the mountainous areas

CHILDREN

Gran Canaria is a great place for children as there are numerous places to entertain them when they tire of the beach or the sun gets too much. Most of the theme parks offer plenty of diversions for adults, too. Close to Playa del Inglés/Maspalomas, and with regular bus services, you will find:

Mundo Aborigen (open daily 9am–6pm), Parque Rural de Ayagaures, Carretera de Fataga Km6, tel: 928 172 295. A re-creation of a Guanche settlement, with life-size models, that is extremely well done.

Camel Safari Park (open daily 9am–6pm), La Baranda, Carretera de Fataga, tel: 928 798 680. Camel treks, a shop and a restaurant are on offer here.

Palmitos Park (open daily 10am–6pm), Carretera de los Palmitos. Ornithological park with parrot shows throughout the day, an aquarium, butterfly house and botanic garden. Adults enjoy it too.

Aquasur (open daily 10am–6pm), Carretera de los Palmitos Km3, tel: 928 140 525. The biggest water park in the Canaries, with slides and flumes of all descriptions.

Sioux City (open Tues–Sun 10am–5pm, plus Fri barbecue at 8pm), Cañon del Águila, San Agustín, tel: 928 762 573. A Wild West theme park, complete with gunfights, bank hold-ups and saloon girls.

Submarine Adventure (daily 10am–5pm), Puerto de Mogán, tel: 928 565 108, takes you on a voyage to the bottom of the sea in a yellow submarine.

Cocodrilo Park (open Sun–Fri 10am–5pm), Los Corralillos, Agüimes, tel: 928 784 725. Parrots, monkeys and deer, as well as crocodiles. This sanctuary is recognised by the local animal protection service, SEPRONA.

In Las Palmas, children usually enjoy a trip around town on the open-topped **Guagua Turística** (tourist bus). You can hop on and off all day at places of interest. Board the bus in Parque Santa Catalina or anywhere en route.

Museo Elder (open Tues–Sun 10am–8pm), the big science and technology museum in Parque Santa Catalina, is usually a hit with children, as there are so many hands-on activities and a section especially designed for very young ones, as well an IMAX cinema.

Palmitos Park has been going for years and is always popular

SHOPPING

Gran Canaria looks set to maintain its status as a Free Trade Zone for the forseeable future, despite membership of the EU, and taxes (IGIC) are low, at 5 percent, so there are savings to be made on tobacco, spirits, perfume, cosmetics, watches, jewellery, and electronic and optical equipment in Las Palmas duty-free shops.

Handicraft items *(artesanía)*, including include textiles, baskets and ceramics, can be found in shops and markets all over the island, but the best quality goods are sold in the outlets of the **Federación para la Etnografía y el Desarrollo de la Artesanía Canaria (FEDAC)**. These are situated at Calle Domingo J. Navarro 7, Las Palmas, tel: 928 369 661; and in the tourist office in Avenida de España, Playa del Inglés, tel: 928 772 445. The FEDAC shops also sell the small knives, once used by banana workers and shepherds, that have become collectors' items. Called *cuchillos canarios* or *naifes*, they have a wide blade and a goathorn handle decorated with inlaid patterns.

Calle Peregrina, just round the corner from the above, has a number of attractive little boutiques and galleries. **Atarecos**, at Calle Peregrina 4, tel: 928 372 628, sells unusual, ethnic-style gifts – scarves, bags and bracelets.

The **Librería del Cabildo Insular** (the official government bookshop) at Calle Cano 24, Las Palmas, tel: 928 381 539, is the place for maps and books about all the Canary Islands.

The airport shop has a wide selection of plants, from miniature dragon trees, to *Strelitzia* (bird of paradise) flowers and a variety of seeds. Whether or not they will grow in the English climate is a gamble, but they make unusual gifts – and there is no restriction on bringing them into the UK.

Embroidered table linen makes a nice souvenir of Gran Canaria

In the big commercial zones of Las Palmas you will find all the major stores, Spanish and international. The biggest centres in Las Palmas are **Las Arenas** (near the Auditorio Kraus), **La Ballena**, in the upper town, and the **Avenida Mesa y López**, which is known as a 'zona comercial', where there are two branches of the biggest Spanish department store, El Corte Inglés. The newest centre, with a wide range of shops as well as cafés, restaurants, cinemas and discos, is **El Muelle**, on the Muelle Santa Catalina.

Among edible items, *queso de flor*, the famous cheese made in Guía, is a good choice. **Santiago Gil Romero**, Calle Marqués del Muni 34, Santa María de Guía, tel: 928 881 875, is the best place to buy it. Jars of *mojo* sauce in many varieties and *bienmesabe* (the almond syrup) are widely available. **La Despensa del Sur**, Calle General Bravo 36, Triana, Las Palmas, tel: 928 360 195, is packed with island wines and local foods.

Markets

Most towns have a market one morning a week, selling food, flowers and household goods. An excellent, and more wide-ranging, one is in **Puerto de Mogán** *(see page 54)*. There's another big one in the San Fernando district of **Playa del Inglés** on Saturday morning. The **Vegueta food market** (open Mon–Thur 6am–2pm, Fri–Sat 6am–3pm) in Las Palmas is a riot of colours and smells and surrounded by tiny, white-tiled bars. Every Sunday morning, a flower market is held in the Plaza de Santa Ana in Las Palmas.

NIGHTLIFE

Discos, clubs and bars fall in and out of favour very rapidly, as they do anywhere else. Very little happens before midnight, so a quiet place you pass at 10.30pm may be jumping 2 hours later. In Las Palmas, Plaza de España in the Mesa y

The Hotel Santa Catalina houses one of the island's two casinos

López district is lively. **Heineken**, at No. 7 is an old favourite, and it's where many people start their evening. **El Coto** in Calle Gomera (basement of Hotel Meliá) is for those who like 1960s music; and **Cuasquias**, Calle Bravo Murillo, plays jazz till late. **La Floridita** (Calle Remedios), is an imitation of the bar of the same name in Havana. Nearby, the café tables in the Plaza Hurtado de Mendoza are full till the early hours. **La Ronería – Museo del Ron** (Calle Secretario Artiles) is a museum dedicated to rum – except that it's only open from 9pm–2am and serves rum-based cocktails.

There are hundreds of bars, clubs and discos of all kinds in Playa del Inglés and Maspalomas. Flyers handed out in the street or listings in local papers will indicate what's available. The commercial centres are the places to go. **Fantasy Island** and **The Garage** are among the biggest and most enduring establishments of the **Kasbah Centre**. The **Yumbo Centre** is known for its gay bars and clubs, the popular **Pub Néstor** among them – although there are numerous straight venues as well.

Casinos: There are two casinos on the island; one is in the luxurious **Hotel Santa Catalina** in Las Palmas (tel: 928 233 908); the other is the **Gran Canaria Casino** (tel: 928 762 724) in Hotel Meliá Tamarindos in San Agustín. Dress smartly and don't forget your passport.

Classical music: The **Auditorio Alfredo Kraus** at the far end of Playa de las Canteras (tel: 928 491 770, bookings 902 405 504, e-mail: info@auditorio-alfredokraus.com) presents excellent concerts by the resident Las Palmas Philharmonic and visiting orchestras, and recitals by top-class soloists. The new **Teatro Cuyás**, Calle Viera y Clavijo s/n, Triana (tel: 928 432 181, bookings 902 405 504), stages world and classical music, dance and theatre. CICCA, Alameda de Colón 1 (tel: 928 368 687/928 373 439, <www.lacajadecanarias.es>) has a varied programme of films, music, modern dance and theatre.

Calendar of Events

6 January: Epifanía del Señor (Epiphany). Children receive their Christmas presents. In Las Palmas the Three Kings (Los Reyes), ride into town, sometimes on camels, throwing sweets to the crowd.

20 January: San Sebastián. Agüimes and Guía celebrate the saint's day.

February: Fiesta de Almendros (Almond Blossom Festival) in Tejeda and Valsequillo (date varies). Traditional handicrafts, dancing and sports displays.

Late February/early March: Carnival. celebrations are particularly outrageous in Las Palmas and Playa del Inglés.

April: Semana Santa. The week preceding Easter is a time of solemn processions.

1 May: Cheese festival Santa María de Guía. Traditional dancing and lots of local produce.

Mid-June: Corpus Christi. The streets of Vegueta and the Plaza de Santa Ana in Las Palmas, and main squares in Arucas and Gáldar, are carpeted with flowers, grasses and coloured sand.

24 June: San Juan (Feast of St John). Dancing, processions, sporting activities in Artenara, Telde, Las Palmas and Arucas.

16 July: Nuestra Señora del Carmen, the patron saint of fishermen, is honoured in all ports, but especially in Arguineguín and Puerto de Mogán where celebrations last at least a week. Statues of the Virgin are taken out to sea in processions of decorated boats.

4 August: Bajada de las Ramas (Bringing down the Branches) is held in Agaete and Puerto de las Nieves. The villagers carry branches from the mountains to the sea and whip the waves.

8 September: Virgen del Pino. Important festival in Teror, which is a mixture of religious rituals and secular fun.

11 September: Fiesta del Charco (Festival of the Lagoon) in Puerto de la Aldea, San Nicolás. Participants try to catch fish with their hands, and duck each other into the water.

Second Saturday in October: Fiestas de la Naval (Festival of the Sea). Maritime processions in Las Palmas and other ports celebrate the victory of the Armada over the English in 1595.

EATING OUT

Canary Islands' food has much in common with that of mainland Spain, but with interesting regional differences. There are also dishes similar to those found in parts of Latin America – although whether these recipes were introduced to the New World by Canarian emigrants, or American inventions brought back by returnees, is debatable.

You will also find many restaurants where the cooking is described as *cocina vasca* (Basque) or *cocina gallega* (Galician) because a number of cooks from these northern regions of Spain have opened restaurants on the island. Their familiarity with Atlantic fish and seafood may help them feel at home here. As these two regions have a reputation for some of the best cooking in Spain, they are a welcome addition.

Fish

As you would expect on an Atlantic island, there is lots of fish and seafood of all kinds. Along with the ubiquitous *sardinas*, fresh from the ocean, the fish most commonly seen on menus are *cherne* (sea bass), *vieja* (parrot fish), *sama* (sea bream) and *bacalao* (salt cod). You will also find *merluza* (hake) *atún* (tuna) and *bonito* (a variety of tuna) and seafood such as *gambas* (prawns), *pulpo* (octopus), *calamares* (squid) and *almejas* (clams).

Eating outdoors in Las Palmas is always a pleasure

Often, fish will be served simply grilled along with

salad, *mojo* sauce and *papas arrugadas (see page 98)* – a perfectly balanced dish – but there are numerous other ways that it may appear on your table. *Sancocho canario* is a popular dish, a stew made with red grouper or sea bass, potatoes and yams, spiced up with a hot variety of *mojo* sauce. *Salpicón de pescado* is another dish you will see on many menus; this is sea bass or grouper cooked, chopped and served cold with a mixture of onions, garlic, tomatoes and peppers, topped with hard boiled egg and olives. A delicacy introduced from the Basque country is *calamares rellenos de bacalao* – small squid with a tasty, cod-based stuffing, sometimes served in a creamy sauce.

Rancho Canario

This is one of the most typical island dishes and, when well made, is delicious as well as filling. Here's how to do it:

300g chickpeas	100g thick vermicelli
150g chorizo	½ glass red wine
125g chicken	1 glass olive oil
100g streaky bacon	½ teaspoon cumin
4 cloves garlic	1 sachet saffron
1 onion	4 sprigs parsley
2 tomatoes	1 tablespoon paprika
1kg potatoes	salt

Soak chickpeas overnight, drain and wash. Bring 1 litre of water to the boil, put in chickpeas, bacon, chicken and chorizo and cook till tender. In a separate pan, heat the oil and fry the onion, garlic, tomatoes, paprika and cumin. Add wine and pour mixture into the chickpea pot, together with the cubed potatoes, salt, saffron and parsley. When potatoes are almost cooked, add the vermicelli and cook for a few minutes. Leave to stand for 15 minutes before eating. Enjoy!

Meat

If you don't like fish, don't despair, there's plenty of meat to be found. *Cabrito* (kid) – sometimes called *baifo* – and *conejo* (rabbit) are most common, but pork (*cerdo*) and chicken (*pollo*) are popular and there are some good steaks to be had in restaurants catering to tourists. Both goat and rabbit are often served *al salmorejo* (with green peppers, in a herb and garlic marinade). *Chorizo* – the red spicy sausage found all over Spain, also crops up in a variety of guises.

Soups

Most of the world's traditional dishes originated as a way of filling stomachs with what was available and inexpensive. In the Canary Islands, this meant a whole range of substantial soups and stews. *Ropa vieja* (literally, old clothes) is a mixture of meat, tomatoes and chick-peas; *puchero* includes meat, pumpkin and any vegetables available; while *rancho canario (see opposite)* is the most elaborate and some say the best. Many of the soups contain chunks of corn on the cob – tasty but not easy to eat in a dignified way.

Vegetarians should be aware that even such innocent sounding dishes as watercress soup *(potaje de berros)*, a staple found on many menus, has chunks of bacon in it. And celery soup *(potaje de apio)* may contain scraps of pork.

Vegetables

The vegetables you are offered will be those that are in season and because the island does not produce a great variety, and imports are expensive, choice may be limited. Pulses such as lentils *(lentejas)* and chickpeas *(garbanzos)* are used a lot; Canary tomatoes are delicious. If you like garlic, ask for *tomates aliñados*, tomato salad smothered with olive oil and garlic. *Pimientos de padrón* – small green peppers cooked whole and covered with salt – originated in Galicia and are now found everywhere. Avocados (strictly speaking a fruit not a vegetable) are served at a perfect stage of ripeness.

Most dishes contain or are accompanied by potatoes *(papas),* and sometimes by *ñame,* a kind of yam. You won't go far without encountering *papas arrugadas* (wrinkled potatoes), which are served with meat and fish or by themselves as tapas. They are small potatoes – the yellow-fleshed Tenerife variety are best – cooked in their skins in salted water then left to dry over a low heat until their skins wrinkle and a salty crust forms. It is said that this dish originated with fishermen who used to boil the potatoes in seawater.

Mojo
Papas arrugadas, and many meat dishes, are usually accompanied by *mojo rojo*, a sauce whose basic ingredients are tomatoes, peppers and paprika. A spicier version *(mojo*

Papas arrugadas **and salad are eaten with both meat and fish**

picón) contains hot chili pepper as well. *Mojo verde* is a green sauce made with oil, vinegar, garlic, coriander and parsley, usually served with fish. The sauces arrive at the table in small bowls so you can use as

> *Trucha* is a word to be careful with. It actually means trout, but *truchas canarias* are almond and aniseed doughnuts, one of the most popular sweet snacks.

much or as little as you like. Every restaurant – and probably every home – seems to have their own version and entire *mojo* recipe books are published.

Gofio

Made of wheat, barley or a mixture of the two, *gofio* was the staple food of the Guanches and still forms an essential part of the diet today – you even see sacks of *gofio para perros* (*gofio* for dogs). The cereal is toasted before being ground into flour and then has a multiplicity of uses. It is stirred into soups and into children's milk and used to thicken sauces. It is made into ice cream and mixed with oil, salt and sugar into a kind of bread, not unlike *polenta*. It is also blended with fish stock to make a thick soup called *gofio escaldado*.

Cheese, Fruit and Desserts

There are only a few Canary Island cheeses, but they are delicious. The best known is a soft cheese, *queso de flor*, which is made in Guía, using a mixture of sheep and cows' milk curdled with the juice of flowers from the cardoon thistle. This won a World Cheese Award in London in 2002, as did the *queso tierno de Valsequillo*, a mild, smooth cheese not unlike mozzarella.

Home grown Canary Island fruit is delicious. As well as the small, local bananas there are papayas, guavas, mangoes and oranges, delicious by themselves, made into juice or used to flavour ice cream. On many menus desserts are limited to ice cream *(helado), flan* (the ubiquitous caramel custard), fresh fruit, and the one you see everywhere, *bienmesabe*, which translates as 'tastes good to me' – and so it does. There are numerous recipes, but basically it is a mixture of crushed almonds, lemon, sugar (lots), cinnamon and egg yolks.

What to Drink

The breakfast drink is coffee. *Café solo* is a small, strong black, like an *espresso*; a *cortado*, always served in a glass, is a shot of coffee with a small amount of hot milk; *café con leche* is a large milky coffee. An *Americano* is a shot of coffee with added hot water. Hot chocolate is sometimes available for breakfast, but if you ask for tea you will just get a teabag in a little pot.

A popular restaurant at Cruz de Tejeda

You are advised not to drink tap water, but *agua mineral* is available everywhere – *con gas* is sparkling, *sin gas* is still. *Zumo de naranja*, freshly-squeezed orange juice, is widely available and in some bars and cafés you can get a variety of more exotic juices.

Wine is usually drunk with meals, most of it imported from the mainland; Rioja is one of the favourites. There are 32 wineries on Gran Canaria, which has a recently introduced Denomination of Origin (DOC), but they come nowhere near to supplying demand. Monte Lentiscal, which has its own DOC, is the most widely available local wine. Tenerife is a bigger producer, but its wines are not regularly found in restaurants.

When Arucas had a thriving sugar industry it also used to be a major centre of rum production. There is still a distillery there, the Destileria Arehucas, producing excellent rum, but sugar has to be imported now so the output is much reduced. Rum forms the basis of *Mejunje*, a local drink in which the spirit is blended with honey and lemon. Another island speciality is *Guindilla*, the cherry liqueur made in San Bartolomé *(see page 77)*.

Beer is extremely popular on the island. You will see familiar Spanish brands such as San Miguel, and other imported beers are available, but the most popular is the locally-produced Tropical.

WHERE TO EAT

When it comes to places to eat, the choice is wide. There are some smart, upmarket restaurants in Las Palmas and Maspalomas that can compete with those in any capital city, and are not expensive by northern European standards. There are fishermen's *tavernas* where the fish is likely to be fresh and wholesome, with very few trimmings; and rural *parillas* – grills – where all kinds of meat and sausage are barbecued over an open fire and served with generous helpings of *papas arrugadas* and *mojo rojo*.

A *piscolabis* is a snack bar serving a variety of little sandwiches and snacks. When you see restaurants advertising *cocina casalinga* – home-cooking – you'll get inexpensive, typically Canarian food, although the quality, of course, can vary. There are not many places that style themselves tapas bars, but in many middle-of-the-range and inexpensive restaurants there will be a variety of tapas on offer, and some of the portions are quite large – two or three would make a meal for most people.

Bars, generally, are places in which to drink, not eat, although most will have croissants or pastries to accompany the morning coffee, some may serve sandwiches *(bocadillos)* or a limited range of tapas. A *kiosco* has the same role and these little kiosks can be found in the main squares of most towns and villages. *(See pages 135–41 for a selection of recommended restaurants.)*

WHEN TO EAT

The islanders, like the people of mainland Spain, eat late. Three o'clock is not an unusual time to sit down to lunch, and ten o'clock is a relatively early hour to start dinner. Some restaurants may close for a few hours between lunch and dinner, but many serve food all day. Those who cater mostly to foreign visitors, aware that habits are different, will have their lunch menus out by midday and serve dinner as early as you like.

Sunday lunch is a major event in Gran Canaria and as this continues throughout the afternoon many restaurants are closed on Sunday evening. Some also close one evening during the week. Because the high season is between November and April, and restaurateurs need to take a holiday, some close completely for three or four weeks in mid-summer.

HANDY TRAVEL TIPS

An A–Z Summary of Practical Information

A

ACCOMMODATION *(Alojamiento)*

Accommodation on Gran Canaria is concentrated mainly in Las Palmas and in large, modern hotels in the southern resorts. Elsewhere, there is not a great deal of choice. You will not find budget accommodation in the resorts; there's only one *pensión* in Playa del Inglés. In Puerto Rico, there are at present no hotels, only apartments, and many must be pre-booked through an agent.

Hotels are rated from one-star to five-star Gran Lujo (GL). Ratings depend largely on facilities; prices within the categories may vary considerably. Prices must, by law, be displayed in hotel reception areas. Breakfast is usually included in the basic rate in the resort hotels and larger establishments. Package holidays tend to be the most economical, offering accommodation in large, comfortable hotels, usually with pools, and in self-catering apartments. Even if you don't want to spend your holiday in the resorts, they can provide a convenient base.

There are also apartments and 'aparthotels', where each room has kitchen facilities yet retains all the trappings of a hotel. Apartments are graded with one to four 'keys' depending on amenities. It is wise to book accommodation in advance, especially during the two high seasons – November to April and July to August.

In the interior of the island there is a growing number of *casas rurales* – rural properties or old town houses that have been converted into small, medium-priced hotels or renovated and rented as self-catering accommodation. For information, contact Turismo Rural de Agüimes, Apartado de Correos 166, Agüimes, tel: 928 124 183, fax: 928 785 988, e-mail: aguimesTR@club.idecnet.com; RETUR (Asociación de Turismo Rural), Calle Lourdes 2, Vega de San Mateo, tel: 928 661 168, fax: 928 661 560, <www.returcanarias.com>; <www.grancanaria.com> tel: 928 462 547, fax 928 460 889; or <www.turismoruralcanarias.com>.

I would like a single/
  double room
	Quisiera una habitación
	  sencilla/doble

With/without bathroom and toilet/shower	**con/sin baño/ducha**
What's the rate per night?	**¿Cuál es el precio por noche?**
Is breakfast included?	**¿Está incluído el desayuno?**

AIRPORT *(Aeopuerto)*

Gran Canaria's Gando airport is on the east coast, about 20km (12 miles) south of Las Palmas. Bus No. 6 goes to Las Palmas (Parque San Telmo and Parque Santa Catalina terminals) every half hour between 6.15am and 8.15pm, then on the hour between 10pm and 2am. The journey takes about 30 minutes and costs €3. There are also hourly buses to Playa del Inglés and Maspalomas between 7am and 10pm (journey time 30–40 minutes), although most visitors going to the resorts will be on package holidays and will be collected at the airport by their tour operator. A taxi from the airport to Las Palmas costs about €20, depending on which part of the city you are going to.

Gando international airport: tel: 928 579 000.

B

BICYCLE HIRE *(Bicicletas de alquiler)*

Bikes can be hired in the resorts. Try Happy Biking, Hotel Continental, Avenida de Italia 2, Playa del Inglés, tel: 928 766 832. For mountain bikes, go to Free Motion, Sandy Beach Hotel, Avenida Aleréces Provisionales, Playa del Inglés, tel: 928 777 479.

BUDGETING FOR YOUR TRIP

Gran Canaria is relatively inexpensive compared with many European destinations. To give you an idea of what to expect, here's a list of some average prices in euros. A euro is currently worth approximately £0.70p and US$1.15.

Accommodation: Rates for two sharing a double room can range from as low as €25–30 at a *pensión* or *hostal* to as much as €400 at a top-of-the-range 5-star hotel. A pleasant 3-star hotel will cost in the range of €80. Rates drop considerably out of season – May to June and September to October are the least expensive – and very pleasant months to be there.

Attractions: Most museums and gardens charge a small entry fee of around €2–3. More expensive are the larger attractions such as Palmitos Park (€16 adults, €11 children); Cocodrilo Park (€9.80 adults, €6.50 children); Aquasur (€15 adults, €10.50 children), but these are places where you can spend at least half a day.

Buses: single trips in Las Palmas, €0.85–€1. Buying a *bono guagua* (book of 10 tickets) cuts the price by about a third. Bus from Playa del Inglés to Las Palmas, €8

Car hire: Including comprehensive insurance and tax, rates are around €35 a day from the big international companies; you get a better deal if you book for a week. There are many competing firms in the resorts that will offer lower rates; and cars booked in advance via the Internet are also cheaper *(see Car Hire)*.

Getting there: Air fares vary enormously, with those from the UK ranging between £150 and £400 (€210–€562). As with hotels, you will get the best deals in May to June and September to October. From the US, flights cost around $960. The cheapest flights are usually available via the Internet, and booked well in advance, or by taking a chance on a last-minute offer.

Meals and drinks: In a bar a continental breakfast (fresh orange juice, coffee and toast or croissant), will cost around €4. The cheapest three-course set meal – the *menú del día* – including one drink, will be around €7–8. The average price of a three-course à la carte meal, including house wine, will be about €25 per person. At the top restaurants you may pay nearly twice that.

Petrol: very cheap by UK standards – around €0.65 a litre.
Taxis: Prices are controlled, and reasonable. From the airport to
Las Palmas the fare is around €20. Most trips within the city, and
around Playa del Inglés, don't cost more than €3.50.

I want to change some pounds/dollars.	**Quiero cambiar libras/dólares.**
Do you accept travellers' cheques?	**¿Acepta usted cheques de viajero?**
Can I pay with this credit card?	**¿Puedo pagar con esta tarjeta de crédito?**

C

CAMPING

There are three official campsites on the island: Pasito Blanco is a
modern, well-equipped site opposite the Pasito Blanco Marina,
with swimming pools, restaurants and children's facilities (first-
class category). Guantanamo, Playa de Tauro, is on the Carretera de
Mogán, Km76. More basic but adequate (third-class category).
Temisas, Lomo de la Cruz, Carretera Agüimes–San Bartolomé de
Tirajana Km34 (third-class category).

CAR HIRE/RENTAL *(Coches de alquiler;* see also DRIVING)

You must be over 21, sometimes 24, to hire a car, and to have held
a valid driving licence for at least 12 months. You need your passport and a major credit card. It is not easy to find a vehicle with
automatic transmission. There are dozens of local companies, especially in Playa del Inglés, where you will be bombarded with
leaflets, and these tend to be cheaper than the international ones. If
you hire a car via the Internet before you leave home, it is also
cheaper *(see Budgeting, above).* Autos Moreno is a tried and tested

local company (central reservations, tel: 928 300 320). The big international companies (Avis, Europcar, Hertz) have offices at the airport, in Las Palmas and in the resorts.

Airport offices:

Avis tel: 928 579 578, <www.avis.com>

Europcar tel: 928 574 244, <www.europcar.com>

Hertz tel: 928 579 577, <www.hertz.com>.

I'd like to rent a car.	**Quisiera alquilar un coche.**
for one day/week.	**por un día/una semana.**
Please include full insurance.	**Haga el favor de incluir el seguro a todo riesgo.**

CLIMATE

In the south of the island sunshine is practically guaranteed all year round. Winter temperatures average 22°–24°C (72–75°F), summer averages are 26°–28°C (79–82°F), although they often exceed 30°(86°F). It can be very windy, even in the hottest months. In the north of the island, temperatures are a few degrees lower and there is more cloud. Higher regions of the mountainous interior, of course, are much cooler. Some rain falls during November to January and in April, but showers are usually short.

CLOTHING

Light summer clothes, sandals and a swimsuit are all you need for much of the time, but bring a sweater or jacket for cooler evenings and for trips to the mountains, and strong shoes if you want to do any walking. A jacket and tie for men and a smart dress for women is appreciated, although not obligatory, in the more expensive restaurants. Don't offend local sensibilities by wearing swimwear or very skimpy clothing in city streets, museums or churches, although you can get away with almost anything in the resorts.

CRIME AND SAFETY

Crime rates are not high, but there is quite a lot of opportunistic bag-snatching and pocket-picking in tourist areas, especially in crowded places such as markets or at fiestas. Robberies from cars are probably the most prevalent, so never leave anything of value in a car. If you have one, use the safe deposit box in your room for valuables, including your passport (carrying a photocopy of your passport is a good idea). Burglaries of holiday apartments do occur, too, so keep doors and windows locked when you are out. You must report all thefts to the local police within 24 hours for your own insurance purposes.

I want to report a theft.	**Quiero denunciar un robo.**

CUSTOMS AND ENTRY REQUIREMENTS *(Aduana)*

Most visitors, including citizens of all EU countries, the USA, Canada, Ireland, Australia and New Zealand, need only a valid passport to enter Gran Canaria. No inoculations are required. Although the islands are part of the EU, there is a restriction on duty-free goods that can be brought back to the UK. The allowance is 200 cigarettes, or 50 cigars or 250g tobacco; 1 litre spirits over 22 percent, or 2 litres under 22 percent and 2 litres of wine.

D

DRIVING

Driving conditions. The rules are the same as in continental Europe: drive on the right, pass on the left, yield right of way to all vehicles coming from your right. Coastal and mountain roads can be extremely sinuous and full of hairpin bends. Use your horn when approaching the sharper bends. In rural areas, be aware that you may come across a herd of goats, a donkey and cart, a large pothole or falling rocks.

Speed limits are 120 km/h (74 mph) on motorways, 100 km/h (62 mph) on dual carriageways, 90 (52mph) on country roads, 50 km/h (31 mph) in built-up areas and 20 (13mph) in residential areas.
Motorways are toll-free.

Traffic and parking: In most towns traffic can be heavy and one-way systems confusing, especially as road signs are often inadequate. Early afternoon (island lunch time) is a good time to get in and out of towns, and you are more likely to find a parking space. It is an offence to park a car facing the traffic. Don't park on white or yellow lines. Blue lines indicate pay-and-display parking areas.

Petrol. Petrol is much cheaper than in the UK and the rest of Europe. Unleaded petrol is *sin plomo*. Some larger petrol stations are open 24 hours and most accept credit cards. In the mountainous centre there are very few petrol stations.

Rules and regulations. Always carry your driving licence with you. It is a good idea to have a photocopy of your passport. Seat belts are compulsory. Children under 10 must travel in the rear.

Road signs. Apart from the standard pictographs you may encounter the following:

Aparcamiento	Parking
Desviación	Detour
Obras	Road works
Peatones	Pedestrians
Peligro	Danger
Salida de camiones	Truck exit
Senso único	One way
Useful expressions:	
¿Se puede aparcar aquí?	Can I park here?
Llénelo, por favor.	Fill the tank please.
Ha habido un accidente.	There has been an accident.

Traffic police. Armed civil guards (Guardia Civil) patrol the roads on motorcycles. In towns the municipal police handle traffic control. If you are fined for a traffic offence, you may have to pay on the spot or take your fine to the local town hall.

E

ELECTRICITY *(Corriente eléctrica)*

220 volts is standard, with continental-style, two-pin sockets. Adapters are available in UK shops and at airports. American 110V appliances will need a transformer.

EMBASSIES AND CONSULATES *(Embajadas y consulados)*

UK: Calle Luís Morote 6, Las Palmas, tel: 928 262 508.
US: Calle Martínez Escobar 3, Oficina 7, Las Palmas, tel: 928 271 259.
Ireland: Calle León y Castillo 195, Las Palmas, tel: 928 297 728.
South Africa: Honorary Consulate, Calle Mendizábal s/n, Las Palmas, tel: 928 333 394.
If you lose your passport, or run into trouble with the authorities or the police, contact your consulate for advice.

Where is the American/British consulate?	**¿Dónde está el consulado americano/británico?**

EMERGENCIES *(Urgencias;* see also EMBASSIES, HEALTH and POLICE)

Here are a few important telephone numbers, which are common to all the islands:
General emergencies: 112
National Police: 091
Local police: 092

Guardia Civil	062
Ambulance:	061
Fire Brigade:	080

Police!	**Policía!**
Help!	**Socorro!**
Fire!	**Fuego!**
Stop!	**Deténgase!**

G

GAY AND LESBIAN TRAVELLERS

Playa del Inglés is very gay-friendly. The Yumbo Centre is the main spot for bars and clubs and the Maspalomas end of the beach is the place to go. There's a Gay Pride Festival in mid-May. Friends of Dorothy Holidays, tel: 0870 609 9699, <www.friendsofdot.com>, cater to the interests of gay travellers of both sexes; or visit <www.gayinspain.com/canarias>.

GETTING TO GRAN CANARIA

By air: There are numerous scheduled and budget airline flights from all UK airports to Gran Canaria. The flight time is 4–4½ hours. Check the web and advertisements in the travel sections of Sunday papers for good flight-only deals. Many people go to the Canaries on all-in package holidays, which can be the cheapest way to do it. For Iberia, the Spanish national carrier, tel: 0845 850 9000, <www.iberiaairlines.co.uk>; British Airways, tel: 0845 773 3377, <www.britishairways.com>; Spanair (now part of Star Alliance group), tel: 0870 6070 555, <www.spanair.es>.

At present there are no direct flights from the USA, but several transatlantic carriers, such as American Airlines, Iberia and Air Europa have flights via Madrid; the overall flight times is about 12 hours. Connections can also be made via London airports; check with a travel agency, or visit <www.opodo.com>.

Inter-island flights are operated by Binter Airlines, tel: 902 391 392/928 579 433, <www.bintercanarias.es>, for information, or book through any travel agency.

By ship: The Trasmediterránea ferry company runs a weekly service from Cádiz to Las Palmas, which takes at least two days. For details, tel: 902 454 645; or contact the website <www. trasmediterranea.es>. Trasmediterránea operates jetfoils to Tenerife from Las Palmas, a trip that takes 80 minutes, and runs ferries to Fuerteventura and Lanzarote (tel: 902 454 645 for general information, 928 273 884 for jetfoils, 928 474 109 for ferries).

The Fred Olsen Shipping Line (tel: 928 495 040, e-mail: reservas@fredolsen.es, <www.fredolsen.es>) runs ferries from Las Palmas to Tenerife six times a day from Puerto de las Nieves (near Agaete) (journey time about 80 minutes; free bus from Parque Santa Catalina). Naviera Armas (tel: 928 300 600 or 928 227 311, <www.naviera-armas.com>) also has regular services to Tenerife, Fuerteventura and Lanzarote. The crossing to Tenerife takes about 2 hours.

H

HEALTH AND MEDICAL CARE

Non-EU visitors should always have private medical insurance, and although there are reciprocal arrangements between EU countries, it is advisable for people from the UK and other member nations to do the same, because the arrangements do not cover all eventualities. The necessary E111 form is available at post offices in the UK. Before being treated it is essential to establish that the doctor or service is working within the Spanish Health Service, otherwise you will be sent elsewhere. Make a photocopy of the form to leave with the hospital or doctor.

Dental treatment is not available under this reciprocal system. Hotel receptionists or private clinics will recommend dentists.

The main hospital in Las Palmas is the **Hospital Insular**, Avenida Marítima del Sur, tel: 928 444 000. The **Red Cross** (Cruz Roja) is based at Calle León y Castillo 231, Las Palmas, tel: 928 290 000.

In the resorts there are numerous private clinics where you will have to pay for treatment on the spot and reclaim it on your medical insurance. The Las Palmeras chain has clinics in Maspalomas, Playa del Inglés and San Agustín; the general 24-hour emergency numbers are: 928 762 992/928 763 366. In Puerto de Mogán, the European Medical Centre, Local 381, tel: 928 56 50 90 is a reputable clinic; in Puerto Rico, the Atlantic Clinic, Calle Doreste y Molina tel: 928 561 355 is one of many, clustered at the entrance to the resort. Most have English-speaking staff.

Most problems visitors experience are due to too much sun, too much alcohol or food that they are unused to. These problems can often be dealt with by **farmácias** (chemists/drugstores). Spanish pharmacists are highly trained and can often dispense medicines over the counter that would need a prescription in the UK. They are open during normal shopping hours; after hours, at least one in each town remains open all night. It is called the *farmácia de guardia* and its location is posted in the window of all other *farmácias* and in the local newspapers.

Where's the nearest (all-night) chemist?	**¿Dónde está la farmácia (de guardia) más cercana?**
I need a doctor/ dentist	**Necesito un médico/ dentista.**
sunburn/ sunstroke	**quemadura del sol/ una insolación**
an upset stomach	**molestias de estómago**

HOLIDAYS *(Días festivos)*

1 January	*Año Nuevo*	New Year's Day
6 January	*Epifanía*	Epiphany
1 May	*Día del Trabajo*	Labour Day
30 May	*Día de las Islas Canarias*	Canary Islands' Day
16 July	*Nuestra Señora del Carmen*	Our Lady of Carmen
25 July	*Santiago Apóstol*	St James' Day
15 August	*Asunción*	Assumption
12 October	*Día de la Hispanidad*	Columbus Day
1 November	*Todos los Santos*	All Saints' Day
6 December	*Dia de la Constitución*	Constitution Day
8 December	*Inmaculada Concepción*	Immaculate Conception
25 December	*Navidad*	Christmas Day

Movable dates:

Carnaval	week of Shrove Tuesday/February or early March
Jueves Santo	Maundy Thursday
Viernes Santo	Good Friday
Corpus Christi	Corpus Christi (mid-June)

L

LANGUAGE *(Idioma, lenguaje)*

The Spanish spoken in the Canary Islands is slightly different from that of the mainland. For instance, islanders don't lisp when they pronounce the letters c or z. A number of Latin American words and expressions are used. The most common are *guagua* (pronounced *wah-wah*), meaning bus, and *papa* (potato). In tourist areas basic English, German and some French is spoken, or at least understood.

The *Berlitz Spanish Phrasebook and Dictionary* covers most of the situations you may encounter during your travels in Spain and the Canary Islands.

| Do you speak English? | ¿Habla usted inglés? |
| I don't speak Spanish. | No hablo español. |

M

MAPS (Planos)

Most tourist offices will give you free maps, which should be sufficient. If you want something more detailed, go to the official government bookshop, Libería del Cabildo Insular, Calle Cano 24, Las Palmas. Be aware that many road numbers have changed and the ones on the new maps aren't always the same as those on the road signs.

| Do you have a map of | ¿Tiene un plano de la |
| the city/island? | a ciudad/isla? |

MEDIA

Radio and television (*radio; televisión*): Many hotels have satellite TV with several stations in various languages, including CNN. TV Canarias is a local station which includes some English language news and tourist information in its programming. English language radio stations include Radio FM 95.3 MHz – Power FM 91.2 MHz – Waves FM 96.8 MHz.

Newspapers and periodicals: Major British and Continental newspapers are on sale in the resorts and Las Palmas on the day of publication. A number of English-language publications have island news and tourist information, but are not evenly distributed. They include *Holiday Gazette & Tourist Guide* (monthly) *Island Sun*, <www.island-sun-newspaper. com> (bi-weekly), *Island Connections* <www.ic-web.com> and various property-based publications.

There is also a good annual restaurant and hotel guide called *¡Qué Bueno!* which is in both English and Spanish.

For anyone who speaks Spanish, the island newspapers are *Canarias7* and *La Provincia: Diario de Las Palmas*. Both of these contain listings of events so they can be useful, even if your Spanish is very sketchy. *El País* and other Spanish national newspapers are also available.

MONEY *(Dinero)*

Currency: The monetary unit in the Canary Islands, as throughout Spain, is the euro, abbreviated €.

Bank notes are available in denominations of €500, 200, 100, 50, 20, 10 and 5. The euro is subdivided into 100 cents and there are coins available for €1 and €2 and for 50, 20, 10, 5, 2 and 1 cent.

Currency exchange. Banks are the preferred place to exchange currency but *casas de cambio* also change money, as do some travel agencies, and these stay open outside banking hours. The larger hotels may also change guests' money, but the rate is slightly less advantageous. Both banks and exchange offices pay less for cash than for travellers' cheques. Always take your passport when you go to change money.

Credit cards. Major international cards are widely recognised, although smaller businesses tend to prefer cash. Visa/Eurocard/MasterCard are most generally accepted. Credit and debit cards, with a PIN number, are also useful for obtaining euros from ATMs – cash machines – which are to be found in all towns and resorts. They offer the most convenient way of obtaining cash and will usually give you the best exchange rate.

Travellers' Cheques. Hotels, shops, restaurants and travel agencies all cash travellers cheques, and so do banks, where you're likely to get a better rate (you will need your passport). It is safest to cash small amounts at a time, thereby keeping some of your holiday funds in cheques, in the hotel safe.

Banking hours are usually Monday–Friday 9am–2pm; large ones may also open on Saturday.

Where's the nearest bank/ currency exchange office?	**¿Dónde está el banco más cercano/la oficina de cambio más cercana?**
I want to change some dollars/pounds.	**Quiero cambiar dólares/ libres esterlina.**
Do you accept travellers' cheques?	**¿Acepta usted cheques de viajero?**
Can I pay with this credit card?	**¿Puedo pagar con esta tarjeta de crédito?**

O

OPENING TIMES *(Horario comercial)*

Shops and offices are usually open Monday to Saturday, 9am–1pm, 4–8pm (although some close on Saturday afternoon). Large supermarkets may stay open all day, as do many shops in the tourist resorts, and some also open on Sunday. Banks usually open Monday to Friday, 9am–2pm; post offices Monday to Saturday, 9am–2pm.

P

POLICE *(Policía)*

There are three police forces in Gran Canaria, as in the rest of Spain. The green-uniformed Guardia Civil (Civil Guard) is the main force. Each town also has its own Policía Municipal (municipal police), whose uniform can vary but is mostly blue and grey. The third force, the Cuerpo Nacional de Policía is a national anti-crime unit that sports a light brown uniform. All police officers are armed. Spanish police are strict but courteous to foreign visitors.

National Police: 091
Local police: 092
Guardia Civil: 062

Where is the nearest police station?	**¿Dónde está la comisaría más cercana?**

POST OFFICE *(Correos)*

Post offices are usually open Monday to Saturday, 9am–2pm. They are for mail and telegrams, not telephone calls. The main post office in Las Palmas is at Avenida Primero de Mayo 62, tel: 928 363 120; in Playa del Inglés, Edificio Mercurio, Avenida de Tirajana, tel: 928 762 341. Stamps *(sellos)* are also sold at any tobacconist's *(estanco)* and by most shops selling postcards. Check <www.correos.es> for information. Mailboxes are painted yellow. If one of the slots is marked *extranjero*, it is for letters abroad.

Where is the (nearest) post office?	**¿Dónde está la oficina de correos (más cercana)?**
A stamp for this letter/postcard, please.	**Por favor, un sello para esta carta/tarjeta.**

PUBLIC TRANSPORT *(Transporte público)*

There is no train service but the bus service is cheap and reliable. In Las Palmas, there are two subterranean bus terminals, in Parque San Telmo and adjacent to Parque Santa Catalina. Tickets on the *guaguas* (buses) cost around €1. A *bono guagua* (pronounced *bono wawa*), a 10-journey ticket, is good value and can be bought in the terminals and in kiosks. City buses run from dawn until about 9.30pm, and there's a night service on major routes.

Most long-distance buses leave from the Parque San Telmo bus station, although some now commence their journeys at the new Santa Catalina terminal. They are run by the Salcai Utinsa company, also known as Global (northern and central routes, tel: 928 360 179/928 368 335; southern routes, tel: 928 381 110/928 372 133;

<www.globalsu.net/es>). *Tarjetas Insulares* are good-value multi-trip tickets for journeys around the island. In Playa del Inglés and Maspalomas services are also efficent, and run to all the main out-of-town attractions. *(For inter-island ferries and flights, see Getting to Gran Canaria.)*

R

RELIGION *(Religión)*

The majority religion is Roman Catholic and church attendance is quite high. Respect people's privacy when visiting churches. There are also Anglican, Muslim, Jewish, Mormon and other religious communities.

T

TAXES *(Impuestos)*

The Impuesto Generalisado Indirecto Canario (IGIC) is levied on all bills at a rate of 5 percent. The tax is not usually included in the price you are quoted for hotel rooms.

TAXIS

The letters SP *(servicio público)* on the front and rear bumpers of a car indicate that it is a taxi. It may also have a green light in the front windscreen or a green sign indicating '*libre*' when it is free. There is no shortage of taxis in urban areas, and there are usually taxi ranks in the main squares. Within towns, the fare is calculated according to the meter; for longer, out-of-town journeys there are fixed tariffs, but you may feel happier if you agree an approximate fare in advance. Taxis are exceptionally good value, with the longest run in Las Pal-

How much is it to the centre of town?   **¿Cuanto es al centro?**

mas costing only around €5; from the airport, the fare is around €20. In the southern resorts, where taxis belong to a local co-operative (tel: 928 766 767), it is also a good, inexpensive way to travel.

TELEPHONE (Teléfono)

Phone booths (kioskos) accept coins and cards (tarjetas telefónicas), available from tobacconists; instructions in English and area/country codes are displayed clearly. International calls are expensive, so have a plentiful supply of coins or use a card. Cabinas – telephone cabins where you make your call then pay at a desk afterwards – are a more convenient way of making long-distance calls. You will find these in Las Palmas (Parque San Telmo bus station, Parque Santa Catalina and elsewhere) and in commercial centres in the resorts.

Calling directly from your hotel room is expensive unless you are using a card from a local long-distance supplier such as AT&T or MCI. Get the free connection number applicable to Spain from the supplier before you leave (they are different for each country).

For international calls, wait for the dial tone, then dial 00, wait for a second tone and dial the country code, area code (minus any initial zero) and the number. International Operator: 025.

Country codes: UK: 44, Ireland: 353, US and Canada: 1, Australia: 61, New Zealand: 64.

Telephone codes for the Canary Islands (which must always be dialled as part of the number, even for local calls): Gran Canaria, Lanzarote and Fuerteventura: 928; Tenerife, El Hierro, La Gomera and La Palma: 922.

TIME ZONES

The time in the Canaries is the same as in the UK, Greenwich Mean Time, but 1 hour behind the rest of Europe, including Spain, and 5 hours ahead of New York. Like the rest of Europe, the islands adopt summer time (putting the clocks forward by an hour) from the end of March through to the end of September.

TIPPING *(Propinas)*

A service charge is often included in restaurant bills (look for the words *servicio incluído*), so an extra tip is not expected. If it is not included, then add around 10 percent, which is also the usual tip for taxi drivers and hairdressers. In bars, customers usually leave a few coins, rounding up the bill. A hotel porter will appreciate €1 for carrying heavy bags to your room; tip hotel maids according to your length of stay.

TOILETS *(Servicios, aseos)*

Toilets in the Canaries are usually called *servicios* or *aseos*, though you may also hear or see the expressions WC *(doobla-vay say)* and *retretes*. Public conveniences are rare, except in bus stations, but most bars and restaurants have lavatories. It is considered polite to buy at least a coffee if you do drop into a bar to use their facilities. Some don't ask questions of casual visitors; other proprietors keep the key behind the bar to make sure their toilets are not used by the general public.

Where are the lavatories?	**¿Dónde están los servicios?**

TOURIST INFORMATION OFFICES *(Oficinas de información turística)*

Tourist offices abroad

Australia: International House, Suite 44, 104 Bathurst Street, PO Box A-675, 2000 Sydney NSW, tel: 02-264 7966.

Canada: 2 Bloor Street West, Suite 3402, Toronto, Ontario M4W 3E2, tel: 1416-961 3131, e-mail: toronto@tourspain.es.

UK: Spanish National Tourist Office, 22–23 Manchester Square, London W1U 3PX, tel: 020 7486 8077, fax: 020 7486 8034, brochure line: 09063 640630, email: info.londres@tourspain.es; www.tourspain.co.uk.

US: 666 Fifth Avenue, New York, NY 10103, tel: 212 265 8822, fax: 212 265 8864, email: oetny@tourspain.es.
8383 Wilshire Boulevard, Suite 960, Beverly Hills, CA 90211, tel: 213-658 7188.

Tourist Offices in Gran Canaria
Most towns have a tourist office, open during normal business hours. Some of the main ones are:
Las Palmas: Patronato de Turismo, Calle León y Castillo 17, tel: 928 219 600, fax: 928 219 601, <www.grancanaria.com>.
Parque San Telmo (kiosk), tel: 928 368 335; Pueblo Canario, tel: 928 243 593.
Agüimes: Plaza San Antonio Abad, tel: 928 783 389.
Gáldar: Plaza de los Heredamientos, tel: 928 895 855.
Maspalomas/Playa del Inglés: Yumbo Centre, Avenida EEUU/Avenida España, tel: 928 771 550/928 762 591.
Plaza de la Constitución 1, tel: 928 723 444.
Puerto de Mogán/Puerto Rico: Lokal 329, Avenida de Mogán, tel: 928 560 029, e-mail: turismo_mogan@teleline.es.

TRAVELLERS WITH DISABILITIES

Gando international airport and most modern hotels have wheelchair access and facilities for travellers with disabilities. Holiday Care is a UK-based organisation that provides information for travellers with disabilities, tel: 01293 774535, <www.holidaycare.org.uk>.

W

WATER *(Agua)*

The island suffers from a water shortage, so try not to waste it. It's best to avoid drinking tap water. Bottled water is available everywhere and is inexpensive. *Con gas* is sparkling, *sin gas* is still. Firgas water, produced in the north of the island, is the nicest.

WEBSITES AND INTERNET CAFÉS

General sites:

<www.grancanaria.com> is the Gran Canaria Patronato de Turismo site.

<www.canary-islands.com> is a search engine for the Canary Islands.

< www.tourspain.es/canarias> the Spanish Tourist Office website.

<www.okspain.org> a branch of the official tourist office site.

For sports and outdoor activities:

<www.solajero.net/aventura>

<www.ocio-rural/actividades>

For information on natural parks and rural tourism:

<www.ecoturismocanarias.com>

<www.grancanariarural.com>

<www.returcanarias.com>

There are dozens of Internet cafés in Las Palmas and Playa del Inglés/Maspalomas, and a growing number in other parts of the island, but they do tend to come and go. In the resorts, you will find them with no trouble in any of the commercial centres. In Las Palmas, a couple of well-established ones are: Dragonbit Comunicaciones, Calle Remedios 4, tel 928 362 124, e-mail: dragonbit@hotmail.com; Cyber Las Palmas, Calle Tomás Morales 56, tel: 928 43 686, e-mail: netgame@retemail.es. Most places charge around €0.60 for half an hour's access, €1–1.30 for an hour.

Recommended Hotels

Accommodation in Gran Canaria can roughly be divided into what you will find in the southern resorts and what is available in the rest of the island. In San Agustín, Playa del Inglés and Maspalomas, accommodation is in large, modern hotels, and many of these are block-booked by tour companies, although an independent traveller can usually find a room. Puerto Rico is an anomaly in that there are no hotels, only apartments, many of which must be booked through a travel agent. Puerto de Mogán is unusual in having a small hotel of character. In Las Palmas there is a wide variety of middle- and upper-priced accommodation, much of it near Playa de las Canteras, but good-quality budget accommodation is harder to find. Outside these areas, a number of rural hotels offer comfortable, medium-priced accommodation in attractive old buildings.

Prices given are for two people sharing a double room in high season. Breakfast is usually included in hotels in the top three brackets; tax (IGIC) at 5 percent is extra (prices should be taken as an approximate guide only).

€€€€	above €180
€€€	€100–180
€€	€50–100
€	below €50

LAS PALMAS

Cantur €€, *Calle Sagasta 28, tel: 928 273 000, fax: 928 272 373, e-mail: cantur@intercom.es*. A welcoming place with a range of facilities, including a crèche, conference rooms, a pool and solarium; and it's only 30m from Las Canteras beach.

Madrid €, *Plazoleta de Cairasco 4, tel: 928 360 664, fax: 928 382 176*. In a pretty little square in Triana, the Madrid has a long history and bags of atmosphere, which more than compensate for the somewhat old-fashioned facilities. It's popular, so book in advance. Rooms facing the square are noisy but fun.

Meliá Las Palmas €€€, *Calle Gomera 6, tel: 928 268 050, fax: 928 268 411, e-mail: melia.laspalmas@solmelia.es*. The largest hotel in town, with 316 rooms, is right on the beach and has all the extras expected of a five-star establishment, including a large pool, cocktail bar, restaurants, a disco, business facilities and parking.

Parque €€, *Muelle de Las Palmas 2, tel: 928 368 000, fax: 928 368 856, e-mail: hparque@idecnet.com*. It's not a beautiful building but it has a very convenient, central location, right beside Parque San Telmo bus terminal, not far from Vegueta. There's a rooftop restaurant, a sauna and steam room. Good value.

Pensión Plaza €, *Calle Luis Morote 16, tel: 928 265 212*. A cut above most of the inexpensive pensions in Las Palmas, the Plaza is right on Parque Santa Catalina. The rooms are clean and functional and those with private bathrooms cost only slightly more than those without. No credit cards.

Reina Isabel €€€, *Calle Alfredo L. Jones 40, tel: 928 260 100, fax: 928 274 558, e-mail: h.reina.isabel@retemail.es*. Recently renovated, and with an excellent location on Playa de las Canteras, the Reina Isabel is a smart and reliably good place to stay. There's a rooftop pool and a gym; and La Parilla restaurant is widely recommended.

Santa Catalina €€€€, *Parque Doramas, Calle León y Castillo 227, tel: 928 243 040, fax: 928 242 764, <www.hotelsantacatalina.com>*. Set in a lush park and founded in 1890, this is the oldest, grandest and most expensive hotel in town. Rooms are furnished with antiques; there's a casino, convention facilities and an excellent restaurant.

Sol Inn Bardinos €€€, *Calle Eduardo Benot 3, tel: 928 266 100, fax: 928 229 139*. This 23-storey tower block has 215 functional rooms. Ask for one on an upper floor: you get a great view, the rooftop swimming pool and restaurant are closer, and the traffic noise is less disturbing.

THE EAST

Agüimes
Casa de los Camellos €€, *Calle Progreso 12, tel: 928 785 003, fax: 928 785 053*. An attractive *turismo rural* hotel built around a shady courtyard, with 12 traditionally furnished en-suite rooms, in the centre of this small town. There is a good restaurant and bar.

Villa de Agüimes €€, *Calle Sol 3, tel: 928 785 003, fax: 928 785 053*. Managed by same company (HECANSA) as the Casa de los Camellos, hence the same contact numbers, this old house with traditional Canarian balcony is very central. Its six rooms, all en suite, are comfortably furnished and have TV and phone.

Santa Brígida
Hotel Escuela Santa Brígida €€€, *Calle Real de Coello 2, tel: 928 355 300, fax: 928 355 701, e-mail: hebs@hecansa.org*. Another member of the prestigious HECANSA chain. The service is excellent and rooms are large and well equipped; there's a pool in pleasant gardens, a gym, sauna and fine restaurant. Good deals available at weekends (Fri–Sat nights).

Hotel Golf Bandama €€, *Lugar de Golf 14, tel: 928 353 354, fax: 928 351 290, <www.step.es/canarias-golf>*. Quite small, with only 25 double rooms, this – as its name implies – is the place for golfers. Tennis and horse riding are also on offer, or you can just enjoy the pool and the scenery.

THE SOUTH

Arguineguín/Patalavaca
La Canaria €€€€, *Barranco de la Verga, tel: 928 150 400, fax: 928 151 003*. A large, luxurious hotel set by the main road and above the sea, with its own sandy beach, exotic garden and attractively landscaped pool. Sea views and plenty of sports facilities.

Maspalomas

Grand Hotel Residencia €€€€, *Avenida del Oasis, tel: 928 723 100, fax: 928 723 108, e-mail: residencia@alweb.es.* This exclusive new hotel consists of traditional-style villas and suites, set in a palm grove 200m/yds from the dunes. Attractive landscaped pool, tropical gardens, gym and thalassotherapy centre.

Maspalomas Oasis €€€€, *Plaza de las Palmeras, tel: 928 141 448, fax: 928 141 192.* This is one of the most luxurious hotels on the island, set in a palm grove just a few metres from the dunes. Beautiful gardens, pools, putting green, tennis courts, billiard room, gym and sauna.

Riu Palace Maspalomas €€€, *Avenida de Tirajana, tel: 928 769 500, fax: 928 769 800, e-mail: rpalacemaspalomas@riu.es.* The Riu chain has at least a dozen hotels on the island. This huge 'Moorish palace' is close to the dunes. Most rooms have sea views, service is excellent; and there's live music several times a week.

Playa del Inglés

Apolo €€€, *Avenida Estados Unidos 28, tel: 928 760 058, fax: 928 763 918, e-mail: apolo@intercom.es.* In a rather noisy location, the Apolo is a long-established, functional four-star hotel. The many facilities include satellite TV, hairdressing salon, Jacuzzi, tennis court, children's playground and conference facilities.

Buenaventura €€, *Calle Gánigo 6, tel: 928 761 650, fax: 928 768 348, e-mail: reservas@creativhotel.com.* This is one of the biggest hotels on the island, with 724 apartments, all with balconies. About 10 minutes' walk from the centre, but there's a free bus to the beach six times a day. Two heated pools and Jacuzzis; six restaurants, serving a wide variety of food; entertainment indoors and out, including karaoke; gym, table tennis and scuba diving school.

Continental €€, *Avenida de Italia 2, tel: 928 760 033, fax: 928 771 484.* Popular with families – it has a crèche during main school holidays – this hotel set in gardens has a pool, sauna, Jacuzzi and massage. There's also a volleyball/basketball court; disco; satellite TV.

Eugenia Victoria €€, *Avenida de Gran Canaria 26, tel: 928 762 500, fax: 928 762 260*. Nine storeys high with marble foyer, this hotel has large, pleasant rooms, wellness centre, big pool, vast breakfasts, children's entertainment and rather impersonal service. About 15-minutes' walk to the beach but there's a frequent, free bus.

Las Margaritas €€, *Avenida de Gran Canaria 38, tel: 928 761 112, fax: 928 765 380*. Another large hotel on this long avenue, close to busy Avenida de Tirajana, Las Margaritas has its own nightclub and well-equipped gym, football and volleyball on sand pitches, and a large pool in a stunning garden.

Parque Tropical €€, *Avenida de Italia 1, tel: 928 774 012, fax: 928 768 137*. This is a modern hotel but constructed in traditional, local style in a relatively quiet location. There's a pleasant garden and pool, petanque, tennis, table tennis, sauna and hairdressing salon.

Riu Don Miguel €€, *Avenida de Tirajana 30, tel: 928 761 508, fax: 928 771 904*. It looks functional, but this is a comfortable hotel, popular with families. Centrally located, although about 10 minutes' walk from the beach. Tennis, volleyball and billiards plus children's playground, pool and entertainment.

Residencia San Fernando €, *Calle La Palma 16, San Fernando, tel: 928 763 906, fax: 928 777 181*. In the working-class San Fernando district, this is the only *pensión* in Playa del Inglés/Maspalomas. Small, basic rooms and shared bathrooms; only worth considering if you're an independent traveller on a very tight budget. No credit cards.

Puerto de Mogán
Club de Mar €€, *Urb. Puerto de Mogán, tel: 928 565 066, fax: 928 565 438, <www.clubdemar.com>*. This pretty little hotel is right on the quayside, so the comfortably furnished rooms have views over the sea and beach or over the port. Friendly atmosphere, lots of personal touches, a small pool and a pleasant restaurant. Also have apartments for rent.

Pensión Eva €, *Lomo Quiebre 35, tel: 928 565 235, fax: 928 569 274*. There are very few *pensións* on the coast, so this is worth a mention. It's on the main road as you drive in; a cheerful little place with shared bathroom, a communal kitchen and laundry facilities. No credit cards.

San Agustín
Gloria Palace €€€, *Calle Las Margaritas s/n, tel: 928 768 300, fax: 928 767 929*. This smart hotel has a poolside bar, tennis courts, mini-golf, a children's playground, a disco, a thalassotherapy centre and an à la carte restaurant.

Meliá Tamarindos €€€€, *Calle Retamas 3, tel: 928 774 090, fax: 928 774 091, e-mail: melia.tamarindo@solmelia.es*. The wide range of sports facilities at this luxurious hotel includes tennis, squash, volleyball and archery. There are also boutiques and conference facilities and one of only two casinos on the island, with everything you need for a spell of indulgence.

THE WEST AND NORTH

Agaete
Princesa Guayarmina €€, *Los Berrazales, tel: 928 898 009, fax: 928 898 525*. Atmospheric old spa hotel situated 8km (5 miles) east of town, in the lush Barranco de Agaete. Run by the same family for three decades, it has a large dining room overlooking the valley, a swimming pool and thalassotherapy treatments (if pre-booked).

Arucas
La Hacienda del Buen Suceso €€€, *Carretera Arucas–Bañaderos Km1, tel: 928 622 945, fax: 928 622 942*. This rural hotel set in a banana plantation just outside town is a fine place to relax. It has a total of 18 rooms, each individually furnished with antiques and with comfortable sofas on shady balconies. There is a pretty courtyard and garden, a small heated swimming pool, a steam room and Jacuzzi, and a pleasant restaurant using locally grown produce with large barbecue area.

Gáldar
Villa Deportiva Hermanos Monzón €€, *Calle Escribano de Écija s/n, Barrial 35460 tel: 928 551 814*. In a suburb off the Sardina road, this friendly place combines modern, comfortable accommodation with a smart sports centre. It has a large restaurant and small bar.

THE CENTRE

Cruz de Tejeda
El Refugio €€, *Cruz de Tejeda s/n, tel: 928 666 513, fax: 928 666 520, e-mail: te&ve@mira-studio.com*. A wonderful place to relax after walking in the Roque Nublo rural park, with a swimming pool and a sauna for tired bones. Just 10 rooms, comfortably furnished, and there's a good restaurant, too.

Fataga
Molino de Agua €–€€, *Carretera Fataga–San Bartolomé Km1, tel: 928 172 089, fax: 928 172 244, <www.molinadefataga. com>*. A rural hotel in a palm grove, close to the restored mill from which it gets its name, this is a peaceful, pleasing place. The restaurant serves authentic local dishes; excursions can be arranged if required.

San Bartolomé de Tirajana
Las Tirajanas €€–€€€, *Calle Oficial Mayor José Rubio s/n, tel: 928 123 000, fax: 928 123 023, <www.hotel-lastirajanas.com>*. A modern, tastefully decorated hotel overlooking the Barranco de Tirajana with heated pool, a restaurant serving authentic Canarian food, and all the facilities you would expect of a four-star hotel, plus peace and quiet and splendid views.

San Mateo
La Cantonera €€–€€€, *Avenida Tinamar 17, tel: 928 661 795, fax: 928 661 777*. Built round the courtyard of a traditional style house, with rustic furnishings. The restaurant uses local produce, and there's a small rural life museum attached. Makes a good base for exploring Tejeda/Roque Nublo.

CASAS RURALES

For a wider selection of rural houses for rent, contact RETUR *(see Accommodation, page 104)*. Price categories are per night for two people but are often lower for stays of a week or more. The minimum stay is usually two nights.

€€€ = over €80; €€ = €60–80; € = under €60.

Agüimes
Casa de las Suárez €€, *Plaza de Santo Domingo, tel: 928 124 183 (rural tourism office)*. Attractive stone house in a pretty square, traditionally furnished; solar-heated water; four double bedrooms.

Casa del Cura €€, *Calle Moral, tel: 928 124 183 (rural tourism office)*. Traditional Canarian house in the town centre; two double bedrooms and a garden.

Moya
Casa Nanita €€, *La Jurada 8, Fontanales, tel: 928 462 547, fax: 928 460 889*. Three separate self-contained units in a rural *finca* 9km (5 miles) from Moya. Swimming pool, garden, barbecue; bikes available.

Teror
Casa Margarita €€, *Calle Padre Cueto 4, tel/fax: 928 350 000 <www.margaritacasaruralcom>*. Opposite the Palacio Episcopal, this 18th-century house has been completely refurbished. It comprises three separate units each with two bedrooms and well-equipped kitchens. Special (higher) rates during the fiesta, in the first two weeks in September.

APARTMENTS AND BUNGALOWS

Price categories are per night for two people in high season but there are good deals to be had at other times. Only a small selection is given, as many can only be booked through a travel agent:

€€€ = over €80; €€ = €60–80; € = under €60.

LAS PALMAS

Brisamar Canteras €€, *Paseo de las Canteras 49, tel: 928 269 400, fax: 928 269 404*. Right on the beach; 41 apartments with TV and phones; shared gardens.

Colón Playa €, *Calle Alfredo L. Jones 45, tel: 928 265 954, fax: 928 265 958*. On the beach; many of the 42 studio apartments have a balcony and sea view.

Playa Dorada €€, *Calle Luís Morote 61, tel: 928 265 100, fax: 928 265 104*. Close to the beach, this is a small block of 20 apartments; TV, phone, wheelchair access.

THE SOUTH

Maspalomas
Duna Flor Maspalomas €, *Avenida T. Neckermann 14, tel: 928 767 675, fax: 928 769 419*. Some 280 bungalows; tennis and squash courts; supermarket; evening entertainment.

Maspalomas Oasis Club €€, *Avenida Air Marín s/n, tel: 928 142 130, fax: 928 142 518*. One hundred bungalows set amid gardens; children's playground; volleyball court.

Playa del Inglés
Broncemar €€, *Calle San Crisóbal de la Laguna 7, tel: 928 773 940, fax: 928 768 573*. There are 193 apartments in this development, with good pools, a tennis court, a children's playground and a supermarket.

Barbados €€, *Avenida de Tirajana 17–19, tel: 928 760 426, fax: 928 765 102*. Sixty-eight apartments in a central but busy location. There is a pool and gardens, a bar and restaurant.

Puerto de Mogán
La Venecia de Canarias €€, *Urb. Puerto de Mogán, Local 328, tel: 928 565 600, fax: 928 565 714, <www.laveneciadecanarias.*

net>. A relatively new and enticing little complex close to the marina; well-furnished apartments with small terraces and good kitchens.

Puerto Rico
Apartamentos El Greco €€, *Avenida Olímpicos Doreste y Molina s/n, tel: 928 560 356, fax: 928 560 037*. Attractively designed and close to the beach; tennis and squash courts. There's a good restaurant attached. Mainly booked by tour operators, so it's best to contact a UK travel agent.

Mayagüez €, *Avenida Lanzarote 22, tel: 928 561 611, fax: 928 561 718*. A small complex – just nine apartments – close to the sea on the Puerto Nuevo side; set in gardens with a pool.

San Agustín
Carolina €€€, *Calle Cardones 3, tel: 928 778 200, fax: 928 778 203, e-mail: sunsuites.carolina@infonegocio.com*. Pretty, white-painted apartments with terraces, pool and lush gardens, close to the beach.

IFA Interclub Atlantic €€€, *Calle Los Jazmines 2, tel: 928 770 200, fax: 928 760 974, e-mail: interclub@ifacanarias.es*. This is the biggest complex in San Agustin, and among the more expensive. It's very popular with watersports enthusiasts, for whom there are good facilities. It has a multipurpose sports court, a crèche and a children's playground. Try for an independent booking, but it's largely in the hands of tour operators.

La Solarena €, *Calle Jazmines 11, tel: 928 763 946*. Reasonably priced, good-value, one-bedroom apartments.

THE NORTH

Agaete
Apartamentos El Angosto €, *Calle Obispo Pildain 11, tel/fax: 928 554 192*. Peaceful, rural location; 12 well-equipped apartments in pleasant gardens, with pool and restaurant, and sea view.

Recommended Restaurants

It is easy to eat well, and relatively cheaply, in Gran Canaria. The capital has a huge choice of eateries, ranging from fish restaurants to those that specialise in typical Canarian dishes, to those with chefs from Galicia and the Basque country, as well as bland 'international' menus. Most northern towns and mountain villages have one recommended place serving local food or grilled meat. In Playa del Inglés, the beachfront is lined with fast-food outlets and others offering inexpensive staples, but the best restaurants are away from the beach, many in Avenida de Tirajana, others in the unprepossessing little San Fernando *barrio*. Ports – such as Puerto de Mogán in the south and Puerto de la Nieves in the northwest – have a plethora of fish restaurants, all offering perfectly acceptable meals at reasonable prices.

Many of the listed restaurants, including some of the more expensive ones, also offer an excellent value *menú del día* – a three-course set menu, including bread and a glass of wine, at remarkably low prices – usually under €8. This is sometimes only available at lunchtime.

Prices (which are only approximate) are for a three-course à la carte meal for one, with house wine.

€€€	€35–50
€€	€20–35
€	below €20

LAS PALMAS

Amaiur €€€, *Calle Pérez Galdós 2, tel: 928 370 717*. Beautifully presented dishes from the Basque country, in a restaurant run for 15 years by a man who knows and loves good food. Small, sweet peppers filled with *bacalao* are among the specialities. Closed Sunday.

El Cerdo Que Ríe €€, *Paseo de las Canteras 31, tel: 928 271 731*. Established in the 1960s when northern European tourists first came to Las Palmas, the Danish-owned 'Laughing Pig' is still extremely popular. Its large menu, written up outside the restaurant, has strong, but not exclusive, Scandinavian leanings.

El Cucharón €€, *Calle Reloj 2, tel: 928 333 296*. In Vegueta, right on the corner of Plaza Santa Ana. The exterior is so discreet you might miss it altogether. Inside, there's elegant décor and authentic island food. Closed Saturday lunchtime, all day Sunday and mid-August to mid-September.

El Herreño €€, *Calle Medizábal 5, tel: 928 310 513*. Close to the Vegueta market, this restaurant is a Las Palmas institution. It serves hearty, simple food from the island of El Hierro, in a relaxed and friendly atmosphere. Large families sit at long tables to enjoy thick seafood stews followed by *gofio* mousse and *bienmesabe*.

El Mordisco €, *Calle San Pedro s/n, Triana, tel: 928 361 127*. A great place for breakfasts, light lunches and all-day snacks and meals, plus fresh fruit juices. Friendly, efficient service; just off Mayor de Triana.

El Padrino €€, *Calle Jesús Nazareno 1, tel: 928 462 094*. This fish restaurant on La Isleta is famous not only for its seafood specialities, but also for marvellous views. Eat indoors or outside in a kind of marquee. Recommended for Sunday lunch. Can be reached by Bus No. 41 from Parque Santa Catalina.

El Patio de Cuyás €, *Teatro Cuyás, Calle Viero y Clavijo s/n, Triana, tel: 928 384 800*. Part of a brand new theatre in Triana. The food is prepared by a well-regarded young chef and shows influences from the many parts of northern Spain in which he has worked. Book for lunch. Closed Monday evening and Sunday.

La Marinera €€, *Plaza de la Puntilla, tel: 928 461 555*. At the end of Playa de las Canteras, this restaurant has a dining room so close to the sea you could almost catch the fish yourself. Fortunately, they do it for you, and cook it extremely well. Barbecued meats are also on offer.

Hipócrates €, *Calle Colón 4, Vegueta, tel: 928 311 171.* Friendly vegetarian restaurant right opposite Casa de Colón. Serves good salads and *gazpacho*, plus more substantial meals in a cool dining room or outside on a little sunny patio with ornamental gnomes. Closed Monday lunch and Sunday evening.

Pepe El Breca €€–€€€, *Calle Prudencia Morales 16, tel: 928 468 791.* The proprietor, who began life as a ship's cook, opened his restaurant in 1962 and has been serving excellent fish and seafood ever since. Try the *ceviche canario* – marinated fish with Herreño cheese. Booking is advisable as Pepe is something of a local institution and the place tends to fill up.

THE EAST

Agüimes
La Oroval €€, *Calle Progreso 12, tel: 928 78 50 03.* One of the high-quality HECANSA chain, this is reached through the inner courtyard of the colonial-style Casa de los Camellos hotel. Traditional Canarian dishes are well presented and the house wine is remarkably good.

Santa Brígida
Mano de Hierro €, *Carretera del Centro Km15, tel: 928 640 388.* Said to be one of the best German restaurants in Spain and very popular with people from Las Palmas. Big on meat, but they also do a very good watercress soup. Open for lunch Tuesday to Sunday, dinner Friday and Saturday.

Bistro Monte €€, *Carretera del Centro 125, tel: 928 351 744.* There's a formal dining room, a fern-filled patio and attractive terrace in this award-winning restaurant. Canarian dishes and local wines are served with pride, and their rice dish, *arroz Bistro Monte*, is a speciality.

Telde
La Posada €€, *Calle Navarra 6, tel: 928 693 623.* Small, friendly, family-run place with rustic decor and good food, especially the

fish. The *merluza con almejas* (hake with clams) is a speciality, and desserts include their own-recipe *gofio* biscuits.

THE SOUTH

Maspalomas

Amaiur €€–€€€, *Avenida T. Neckermann (opposite the golf club)*, tel: 928 764 414. Run by the brother of the Las Palmas Amaiur proprietor, with the same attention to quality and detail, albeit a slightly more international menu. *Rape en salsa verde con gambas* (monkfish in green sauce with prawns) is delicious.

La Casa Vieja €–€€, *Carretera de Fataga 139, tel: 928 769 010*. Traditional food served in an old country house with rustic decor and cane-lined walls, just a short taxi ride from the tourist centres. Barbecued meat and goat stews are among their specialities.

Le Provençal €€, *Avenida T. Neckermann (opposite the golf club)*, tel: 928 765 107. Next door to Amaiur, this family-run restaurant, with bright Provençal tablecloths and lots of flowers, serves good quality French food such as rabbit with coriander *(conejo al cilantro)* and a variety of terrines.

Pepe El Breca II €€, *Carretera de Fataga, tel: 928 772 637*. Sister of the Las Palmas restaurant, this one is run by Pepe's daughter, using the recipes her father made popular. The sea bass baked in salt is excellent – and, no, it's not salty. Also features typical Canarian desserts. Slightly off the beaten track, but well worth the journey.

Mogán

Casa Enrique €–€€, *Calle San José 3, tel: 928 569 542*. Big, rather old-fashioned looking place in the main street where the proprietor serves local food such as *puchero* and *rancho canario (see page 96)* as well as plain grilled fish and steaks.

Mesón Stéphane €€, *Calle San José 1, tel: 928 569 316*. Next door to the above, Stéphane is a chic little place with a wood-fired oven on the terrace overlooking the valley. French influenced menu includes *lapin chausseur* and *escargots*. Closed Wednesday.

Playa del Inglés
Compostela €€, *Calle Alcalde Marcial Franco 14, tel: 928 763 344*. As the name would suggest, the emphasis here is on food from Galicia. Specialities include *merluza a la Bilbaina* (hake, Bilbao style), served in an airy restaurant with nautical touches in the San Fernando district.

Las Cumbres €€, *Avenida de Tirajana 11, tel: 928 760 941*. This long-standing favourite is decorated with old agricultural and domestic utensils. It specialises in dishes from various regions of Spain, particularly slow-roasted lamb, splendid Iberian hams and prawns from Huelva. Closed Tuesday and all of May.

Restaurante Riche €, *Jardín del Sol, Avenida de Gran Canaria, tel: 928 769 733*. Easy to miss as it's tucked slightly off the main road, but worth a visit for good quality, inexpensive food. A variety of tapas is on offer, too, and service is helpful and friendly.

Tenderete II €€, *Edificio Aloe, Avenida de Tirajana 15, tel: 928 761 460*. On the ground floor of an apartment block, this doesn't look much from outside, but has been consistently good and popular for many years. Specialises in island dishes such as *puchero* and *rancho canario (see page 96)*. Reservations recommended.

Puerto de Mogán
La Bodeguilla Juananá €€, *Puerto Deportivo, tel: 928 565 044*. Tucked in a little square just off the quayside, this tiny place is festooned with hams, peppers and fruit. It specialises in Canarian food, including island cheeses and wines, plus a good selection of Iberian *charcuterie (embutidos)*.

La Cofradía €€, *Dársena Exterior s/n, tel: 928 565 321*. This is a local favourite on the fishermen's quay, where the fish comes straight off the boats. Busy and fun at Sunday lunchtime. If you're splashing out, go for the *cazuela de langosta* (lobster casserole).

Puerto Rico

Picasso €€, *Europa Centre, tel: 928 560 041*. You will need to get a taxi as it's right at the top of the hill. The menu features mainly seafood, fish and steaks, all well prepared and good value.

Red Rose €€, *Puerto Nuevo, tel: 928 562 185*. No view of the port although it's only a stone's throw away. Specials such as duck with orange sauce and lobster and seafood platter must be ordered 24 hours in advance. Popular with the English ex-pat community.

THE WEST AND NORTH

Agaete

Casa Romántica €–€€, *El Valle de Agaete, Km3.5, tel: 928 898 084*. Swiss owned, this attractive place has a lush tropical garden and large dining areas – sometimes taken over by tour groups. The menu includes creamed pumpkin soup and steak in red wine sauce. Closed Monday and Tuesday.

Moya

El Gallo €€, *El Palmital, Santa María de Guía, Carretera Moya–Guía Km32, tel: 928 559 139*. Outside the town, on the way to Los Tilos de Moya forest, this large cheerful place serves many products grown or raised on its own organic farm. Closed Monday and Tuesday.

Puerto de las Nieves

El Dedo de Dios €€, *Puerto de las Nieves, tel: 928 898 000*. The best known of the fish restaurants in this little port. Named after the finger of rock behind it, and overlooking the sea, it serves good fresh fish and seafood in a large, busy and efficently-run dining room.

Las Nasas €€, *Calle Nuestra Señora de las Nieves 6, tel: 928 898 650*. One of a row of fish restaurants overlooking the port, Las Nasas has a cavernous dining room and an open terrace. They make a version of *ropa vieja* with octopus *(pulpo)*. Popular with Las Palmas weekend visitors.

Teror
El Secuestro €–€€, *Avenida Cabildo Insular 26, tel: 928 630 231.*
This is a reliably good *parilla* overlooking the town, where they
barbecue every kind of meat or sausage imaginable amid rustic
decor in a cheery atmosphere. Good fun at Sunday lunchtime.
Closed Sunday evening and Monday.

THE CENTRE

Artenara
Mesón La Silla €, *tel: 928 666 108.* This is the famous cave
restaurant, with spectacular views from its sunny terrace, and
kitchens cut into the rock. It serves typical, robust meat dishes,
many with *mojo* sauce. Closes at sunset.

San Mateo
El Fogón de la Magua €€, *Hotel La Cantonera, Avenida de Tinamar, tel: 928 661 795.* Part of a rural hotel *(see page 131).* Farm
implements adorn the open patio, local produce features on the
menu, and there's a good cellar that includes island wines. Popular
with tour groups, who visit the attached rural life museum.

Santa Lucía
Restaurant Hao €, *Calle Tomás Arroyo Cardosa, tel: 928 798 007.*
Typical *parilla* on the main road as you enter the village. Serves fresh
kid *(cabrito)* from the grill in a gregarious atmosphere at long plank
tables. There is a small archaeological museum attached.

Tejeda
El Refugio €, *Cruz de Tejeda, tel: 928 666 188.* You can eat
indoors or on the roof terrace. Roast meats, such as goat and rabbit,
are specialities but there are also good salads if you want a lighter
meal. Excellent value and superb views across the mountains.

Yolanda €–€€, *Cruz de Tejeda, tel: 928 666 276.* Next door to the
above, this is a smaller place that also serves good value *asados*
(roast meats) as well as salads, soups and sandwiches. A small covered terrace gives views of Tenerife's El Teide on a clear day.

The world's largest collection of visual travel guides

• • • • • • • • • •

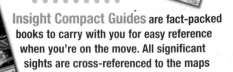

Insight Guides provide the complete picture, with expert cultural background, remarkable photography and full coverage of sights and attractions

• • • • • • • • • •

Insight Pocket Guides highlight an author's personal recommendations for the best things to see and do on a short visit. They include a large fold-out map

• • • • • • • • • •

Insight Compact Guides are fact-packed books to carry with you for easy reference when you're on the move. All significant sights are cross-referenced to the maps

• • • • • • • • • •

Berlitz Pocket Guides put the world in your pocket with detailed information, an easy-to-use A–Z of practical advice, eye-catching photography and clear maps